Stop Being a
VICTIM

Forge Books by Junius Podrug

FICTION

Presumed Guilty
Frost of Heaven

NONFICTION

Stop Being a Victim

Stop Being a VICTIM

Junius Podrug

A TOM DOHERTY ASSOCIATES BOOK
NEW YORK

Designed by Nancy Resnick

A Forge Book
Published by Tom Doherty Associates, Inc.
175 Fifth Avenue
New York, NY 10010

Forge® is a registered trademark of Tom Doherty Associates, Inc.

Library of Congress Cataloging-in-Publication Data

Podrug, Junius.
    Stop being a victim / Junius Podrug.—1st ed.
       p.   cm.
    "A Forge book."
    Includes index.
    ISBN 0-312-86845-6 (alk. paper)
    1. Crime prevention.   2. Safety education.   3. Security systems.
    4. Self-defense for children.   I. Title.
HV7431.P63   1998
364.4'0457—dc21   98-26464
                                              CIP

First Edition: November 1998

Printed in the United States of America

0 9 8 7 6 5 4 3 2 1

For Angela Podrug,
Elizabeth Krische,
Helen Gleason,
and Genevieve McCleary,
tough women who survived a man's world.

Contents

Contents

PART I

Alarming Our Lives and Not Just Our Cars

Land of the free and home of the brave. And you'd better be damn brave here, because people are free to do pretty much anything they like. Behind white picket fences and two-car garages, husbands clobber their wives silly while their kids make crack deals over the phone with Scarface *on the tube.*

—Fielding's, *The World's Most Dangerous Places*

1

We Are All Victims

*In the end each man kills himself in his own
select way, fast or slow, soon or late.*

—Karl Menninger, *Man Against Himself*

We are all victims. The best of us. The smartest. The fastest
and the tallest. None of us are immune. Why? Because *Future
Shock* is here. Everything is accelerating—in this multi-
faceted, complex society we are hit with so many different
hurdles to jump, we too often let others be in control of our
lives and our emotions because we just can't cope with all of
the situations that can arise. There's something new every
day, and the "rules" keep changing, especially at work and
in relationships.

I've had an opportunity to see all sides of the victimization of people, from my youth as a high-school dropout to
seven years of college and being a Los Angeles lawyer who
has represented and watched important and successful
people, CEOs of major corporations and celebrities make
themselves victims. After dealing with thousands of victims
and criminals, listening and talking to people from every

state during appearances on national radio and television shows, I have learned that we inadvertently create the *opportunity* for so many of the terrible things that happen.

Let me give you an example.

While I was driving a client to court a rude jerk nearly caused a collision and I started to honk my horn, but the young woman with me begged me not to—and told me why. The story has a lot to do about guys who think their car is an extension of their penis.

Two months earlier, returning from having a hamburger with friends, she was in a car with her boyfriend. In the car ahead were her girlfriend Jenny and Jenny's boyfriend, Jack. It was early evening, about ten o'clock, when a car came up behind them. The road had one lane in each direction and, with oncoming traffic, there was no passing. The car behind them tailgated the car my young friend and her boyfriend were in and hit the brights. The rude bastard in the car was signaling for them to pull over so he could pass. The boyfriend did exactly that, pulling toward the shoulder to let the creep pass and he proceeded ahead of them, moving up to tailgate Jack and Jenny, giving them the brights and honking his horn.

But Jack wasn't as compliant . . . instead of pulling over, he started playing road games, swerving to make it hard for the other car to pass and hitting the brakes to cause the creep to slam on his brakes. When the creep finally got the chance to pass, he did it on the passenger side. Pulling up beside the car, he fired a shot into the car that struck Jenny in the spine and paralyzed her.

Jenny is in a wheelchair because she met up with a crazy. But we have to wonder what might have happened if Jack hadn't been such a cool dude that he was willing to risk taking on a crazy and proving that he couldn't be pushed around.

I know nothing about Jack—maybe he has all the colors of the rainbow in karate belts, is a crack shot or a college football hero, but what good did any of that do Jenny the night he decided to take on a nut with a gun? There was a nightmare on the road looking for somewhere to land, and Jack gave him the opportunity.

And Jenny did something we all do too often—*she put her life in someone else's hands.* Jack was bigger and stronger than she, they were in his two-thousand-pound car, and dealing with this road trash was a "man" thing. Rather than insisting that Jack knock it off, she created an opportunity to be made a victim.

Some of the smartest people we know put their trust in the wrong person. *Look at Princess Diana.* She assumed her driver, her bodyguard, and her boyfriend would take responsibility for making sure no harm would come to her. Now she is dead.

We have to face the fact that nothing is secure anymore. Nothing is forever. Not our jobs. Not our relationships. Maybe not even our happiness. And most certainly, *not our lives.* The prime objective in an age in which crime has become full of mindless rage and violence, in which the human spirit is being displaced by computer chips, and even the swiftest and the bravest can barely keep up with "progress," is to survive, physically, emotionally, and financially with our dignity and humanity intact.

We can either change to the new conditions or spend our lives as victims. Fortunately we can think, we can stir our brain juices and awaken age-old survival instincts to adjust to the new reality and modify behavior. When a mink is caught in a trap, it will chew off its own leg to escape. That is the most courageous act of personal responsibility that I know. But we don't have to self-mutilate ourselves because we can think our way out of life's traps.

We just need some basic tools to use. Providing those tools is the purpose of this book.

We have learned how to read food labels for the fat content and understand the need for exercise for good health, but most of us are still inept when it comes to dealing with the problems in our own family, buying a car, straightening out a mistake at the bank, hassling with problems—and troublemakers—at work, or taking care of our personal safety so we don't get mugged or raped in the parking lot of the health-food store we shop at to make sure we lead a long healthy life.

I was ripped off buying my first car, have been hassled at work by creditors for someone else's debts, had a gun against my stomach and have been so exasperated by the impersonal clerk on the 800 number to my bank that I can understand why some people go through an emotional meltdown dealing with a trivial problem with their bank or credit-card company. I've represented women who have been raped emotionally and physically—and I've had the unpleasant duty to deal with the bastards who did it. I've fought for men who have been cheated and humiliated—and took on crooks who did it to them.

And something I have learned from over twenty years of experience is that most of us make ourselves victims by giving others the *opportunity* to rip us off emotionally or financially. For example, when I bought my first car, I thought the salesmen were honest and wanted to help. I drove onto a lot on the way home from work with a decent car on a dark and rainy night and drove out with a battered one that had a driver's side window that wouldn't roll up. As I drove home with water spraying in my face from the open window, I knew I had been screwed. The next morning I discovered the black car had once been pink and the front grill was missing. Because I was young and naive, I created the opportunity for a used-car thug and his closer to take advantage of me.

Everyone has to learn and keep up with the constantly changing "rules" on how to buy a car, a house, or dealing with the impersonal and often senseless way we are treated by our bank and other services we *pay* for.

We need to know the "rules" on how to cope with an abusive supervisor at work or with the jerk at the next desk who brings their problems in to the job so we can all suffer.

We need to understand that our emotions blind us in our relationships and families, enabling others to turn us into victims when we take up the slack because they have abandoned their responsibilities or expect us to provide for their happiness.

Coddled by a false sense of security in a society in which crime is a raging plague, we are victimized and intimidated on the streets and not secure in our own homes because we have been so spoon-fed that we've lost some of our "street smarts" and "people smarts."

My mother was both street-smart and people smart. She only had a fifth-grade education, but she had a degree in hard knocks. The day after I bought that pink-black car, she shoved the car down the dealer's throat, letting them have a choice of keeping the car or keeping their license. I watched her and learned (as my wife and I were leaving the showroom after buying my last car, the salesman who tried to screw me stepped in front of me and told me I cost him his job—I told him that was good, now I'd get his license).

Few of us have the quick retorts my mother had in dealing with problems. When I was a kid and the gas company turned off our heat just before Christmas because we couldn't pay the bill, my mother called the manager and told him that unless they turned the heat back on, she was going to rob a bank and tell the newspaper that she did it because the gas company was freezing her children. We had the manager and a worker to turn on the gas out to the house, pronto.

We live in a different world than my mother did, and our responses need to be different—if you called the gas company today to threaten to rob a bank, instead of a "manager," you'd get a clerk at a computer terminal who can't deal with the problem because kids freezing around the Christmas tree isn't covered by the job manual. And when the clerk hears you make a threat to rob a bank, a button gets pressed that automatically dials the *SWAT* team. . . .

While few of us have that killer instinct that my mother had for cutting aggressors off at the knees, we can learn techniques that will keep most agressors at bay.

We have to realize that we are vulnerable because we love too much, hurt too much, and give too much. Most people are decent and hardworking; they wouldn't rip off their neighbor or act like they have a company manual for a brain and a computer chip for a heart. We don't try to rip off other people, and it comes as a shock when we get ripped off by them.

Getting financially scalped in a divorce is an example of how all of us, whether it is in a divorce or in some other emotionally charged situation at home or at work, make victims of ourselves.

I was on a talk show when a woman called in to let the world know that because of lawyers she has been subjected to a bitter divorce battle. I can't count the times I've heard this story. In the chapter on divorce, you'll learn that I rate most divorce lawyers as bottom feeders. But I wanted to grab the woman over the airwaves and shake her and tell her that *she* created the opportunity to be victimized. She and her husband turned themselves into victims by letting high-priced strangers take charge of their emotionally packed relationship. When they walked into their respective lawyer's office, full of anger and hurt, they had a sign hanging from their neck that said, "Take advantage of me because I'm not in control of my life."

We're human—the question is not whether we are going to make mistakes, but whether we will learn from our mistakes and stop giving others the opportunity to make us victims.

Take employment. There was a time when you gave your life to the company, and they gave you back something. But companies don't give a damn about loyalty anymore because they are too big, too impersonal, and people in charge believe no one is indispensable (except themselves, of course). It doesn't matter if you are working for the government, a Fortune 100 company, or a mama-papa outfit; neither you nor your future is secure. And sometimes you're subject to the most arbitrary and capricious acts.

I get infuriated when a man or woman comes to me with a work problem, and I hear stories that sound like things aren't going well for someone else at work, usually a boss, and that person is taking it out on others. What bothers me most is how often the client will not know how to deal with the situation and is making it worse by giving the opportunity for the supervisor to victimize them.

Here's a typical scenario from my client Mary. She works for a large company, has been there three years, and plans to work there forever. But things changed. She got a new boss, and there is a "personality" clash. And the boss started riding Mary, who already has enough problems in just getting her kids off to school each morning and dealing with an ex who is late with everything.

Mary's response to the new environment at work was to let her emotions take control of the way she dealt with the flack, alternately becoming angry and stressed-out, and staying home "sick." When she resorted to emotions to deal with the situation, she lost the war because instead of stopping the problem or making it manageable, she opened herself up to more opportunities to be victimized. I've laid out a number of these situations in the chapter on dealing with problems at work, but there is a common denominator to the advice—*don't play into the hands of the tormentor.*

When to open our mouth or keep it shut, when to be the squeaky wheel, how to find out what our rights are in the company and how to enforce these rights are things that even the sharpest employees at the company usually don't know because dealing with emotional abuse isn't part of the job description or the training received.

Getting control over an emotionally charged situation at work isn't much different than doing it in a divorce or other relationship crisis, dealing with a clerk on the 800 line, or even with street trash who want your money *and* your life. I've talked a nut with a gun against my stomach into not killing me, I've stood before a court and argued for justice, triumphed over the clerk on the 800 number, and dealt with the salesman who dropped the ball on the sale of our house, and I've learned that there are a few basic responses that cover almost any situation.

I also learned that you take responsibility for your own life and don't put it into someone else's hands just because you trust them.

Psychiatrist Karl Menninger theorized that many people set out to victimize themselves, to literally sabotage their lives, by excessive drinking, smoking, screwing up at work, putting themselves into financial ruin, or permitting others to take advantage of them. While most of us are not consciously self-destructive, we do things unconsciously that turn us into victims. One of my clients was raped because she left her security to a motel maid. The poor woman created the opportunity for the rapist by assuming, *trusting,* that the maid locked the bathroom window.

My sister and brother-in-law are wonderful people. The salt of the earth. Loving. Successful. But they drive me crazy because they have paid to alarm both their *insured* cars . . . but not their *lives.* One day my sister was coming in the front door with her two kids when an intruder, who heard them entering, rushed out the back with some jewelry. She missed a potentially deadly confrontation by seconds. They still have their fifteen-thousand-dollar cars alarmed, but they have never alarmed their house—and while there are over a million car thefts a year, there are almost *twice* that many home burglaries. They don't even bother with ninety-nine-cent hardware that keeps intruders from lifting out sliding windows and doors.

Who exactly is in charge of their security? The police? Their neighbors? The crank addict two doors down? What does it take for a wake-up call—a personal tragedy that can never be remedied and never forgotten?

Keep this in mind: the car salesman who talks us into paying an extra thousand dollars, the person at work who makes our lives miserable because theirs is so damn miserable and they need someone to beat on, the street trash with a knife at our throat, all have one thing in common: *they are opportunists, and we created the opportunity.*

We are a nation of victims who go through life threading a minefield of rip-offs and hassles, from buying a car or a home, to dealing with the jerk at work who sorely needs an attitude adjustment, or getting *into* a divorce or *out* of a relationship. The victimization of America carries from the streets and into our homes, where we have turned control of our lives and responsibility for our safety and happiness over to people who aren't going to be there when we need them.

How did we get into this victim mode?

Our reactions to everyday problems are a product of a lifetime of conditioning, and to get out of the victim mentality we need to change. People are naturally resistant to change, but we can change if we are motivated. A fifty-year-old man is suddenly able to give up smoking and fatty foods—despite thirty years of food abuse and endless Surgeon General warnings.

Like so many people, I needed a wake-up call before I would stop creating the opportunity for family and friends—and car salesmen and other thugs—to turn me into a victim.

Getting *street*-smart—*people* smart—is a state of mind that comes from some basic tools. It's learned by getting exposed to problems—and you will be exposed to hundreds of situations as you go through this book. We will discuss many types of victims, what makes us victims, and how to prevent becoming a victim.

Once you've applied some simple techniques, you will be able to deal with almost any type of problem in an automatic and effective manner, using the same type of verbal and physical responses whether you're dealing with that computer operator on the 800 number to your bank, an in-your-face supervisor at work, a fast-talking salesman, or a crazy with a gun.

Teddy Roosevelt, who led a battle charge one day and ran the country the next, gave advice in 1901 that is as good today as it was a hundred years ago: *Speak softly . . . and carry a big stick.*

America was a stronger and brighter place when President Roosevelt gave that advice. But each of us has the same potential to be as strong in the coming millennium as Americans were at the turn of the past century. We just need to awaken skills and instincts about dealing with situations and people, treading softly but being ready to stand up for our rights.

PART II

Protecting Your Job, Relationships, and Money

There are people who eat the earth and eat all of the people on it like in the Bible with the locusts. And other people who stand around and watch them eat.

—Lillian Hellman, *The Little Foxes*

No one can make you feel inferior without your consent.

—Eleanor Roosevelt, *This Is My Story*

2

Getting *People* Smart

We all have our list of wants, even if the list is only in our heads. We want a life partner or want the one we have to love us, we want approval at work, respect from our kids, good interaction with family. When we need a lawyer, have an insurance claim, need to deal with a doctor for a serious medical problem, or seem to have the whole world on our back, we want good results. Few of us have the "people" skills to get all of our wants, but *most* of us can get what we want *most* of the time if we know how to go about it. All of us have these skills to one extent or another, but need to sharpen them in this complex world where "they" keep changing the rules.

The following is a list of the most common mistakes that prevent most of us from reaching our goals, whether it is dealing with those we love, those we wish to persuade to believe in us (the boss at work, your lawyer in a divorce), or simply someone you need something from (the person handling your insurance claim, the service advisor handling your car problem).

1. *People often don't recognize the nature of the problem they are facing.* They know what they want—but haven't defined why they are not able to get it. Overweight persons who want to be thin know they eat the wrong things—but few define *why* they can't accomplish their goal. It doesn't matter if the problem is in our body, our work, our relationships, or just something called life . . . the scenarios are endless but there is a common denominator in successfully dealing with them: We have to direct ourselves at the source of the problem or we will not be able to get the result we want. There is an old expression about seeing the forest from the trees—we need to step back and out of ourselves and look at the problem

2. *We don't define what the other person requires from us.* We have to recognize that the other person has needs, whether it is someone we love or an adjuster from the insurance company filling out a form, we have to give them what they need in order to get what we want. A good example is hassling over a new car that has turned out to be a lemon. Many of us fail unnecessarily in these negotiations because we do not understand the manufacturer's requirements that have to be met.

In dealing with people not in our "inner circle" we have to keep in mind that they are working off of a set of rules, and we have to know what they need from us to give us what we want. Knowing what the rules are keeps us from creating opportunities for others to victimize us.

3. *We make inappropriate emotional responses to situations.* Our spouse in a divorce does something nasty. We reply emotionally by striking back. Our boss criticizes our work, and we go to pieces. Our car is a lemon—we don't find out what the criteria are to qualify for relief but expect

to get "justice." We are angry at the insurance company, angry at our boss, angry at the phone company, at our credit-card providers. Our son or daughter gets into drugs or trouble and we are angry at the school and angry at their friends. Some of the anger may be well placed, but we lose our cutting edge to win when we surrender to emotions. And we turn off the person we're dealing with.

4. *We paint the other person into a corner.* This is the most frequent sin of negotiating that I know of, and we are just as guilty at doing it in personal relationships. What happens is that we make ultimatums or take positions that are deal-breakers or relationship-breakers because the other party cannot or will not meet the terms. It may be that the issue is nonnegotiable, that there is nothing that will bring us and them together, but what I've frequently seen in thousands of negotiations is one side making demands that could not be met.

5. *We don't go to the right person to get what we want.* It does no good to chew out a clerk on an 800 number, a claims adjuster, or the person stocking the shelves down at the supermarket, but people do it all of the time. If you want something, get to a level where you can get results. This can be done by courteously and politely asking the person you are dealing with for their supervisor—and that person's supervisor, right up to the top until we get the response we want.

6. *We blame others for the bad decisions we make.* We all make choices and some of them burn us. It's easy to shift the blame, but when we do we keep on making the same mistakes. We have to learn from our mistakes by taking responsibility and modifying our behavior.

7. *We don't listen.* People talk more than they look and listen. And often they don't know how their actions are affecting others. Fortunately most of us have enough people

skills to understand when we are shooting ourselves in the foot, but there are people who do not have a clue because they are so full of themselves that they don't know how they are affecting others. Getting too wrapped up in how wonderful we are or how worthless we are or how many problems we have affects the people we want results from. This isn't just a social problem—people frequently destroy their careers by not recognizing the signals being sent.

Bottom line, it's the process of how we go about getting our wants and needs fulfilled that we need to keep sharp. Too often we are so engrossed in the final result of what we want to accomplish that we don't realize the damage we do in the process.

When I was a new lawyer I once made the mistake of telling a judge that a situation wasn't "fair" and got an angry response because the law isn't about being fair, it's a set of rules we have to abide by, and "fairness" isn't always the name of the game. Law is just a reflection of life. Bad things happen to nice people. The only thing we can do is try to have as many good things happen to us and those we love and sidestep as many bad ones as we are able.

In dealing with people we should treat others fairly and reasonably and not to try to take advantage of them. What is ours, is ours, and life is too short to spend it coveting what others have. Unfortunately, there are too many people in this world who want more from us than they are entitled to. Sometimes they want our money—or they just try to suck out our emotional marrow. When that happens, we should handle the situation with reason and logic because any other method gives them the opportunity to victimize us.

And when reason and logic just won't work, don't forget that wonderful biblical adage about "doing unto others as you would have them do unto you." An addendum needs to be added for dealing with people who have no redeeming social value: *Do onto others as they deserve.* There are some people in this world who just can't be dealt with on a logical and reasonable basis.

My mother was a simple woman with little formal education, but she had wonderful instincts about dealing with people, not to mention a great deal of wit and wisdom. Sometimes when I came home at night I would find the neighborhood people gathered around her in the living room discussing their problems.

She also knew that there was only so much you can take before you stand up for your rights. There was a Woolworth's store in town and when my mother went into it, something about her attracted the attention of a cranky clerk who would follow her around as if my mother was a thief. This was a wrong call by the clerk—if my mother found a dollar on the street she wouldn't rest until she located the owner. She was offended by the person's attitude and suspected that it arose because we lived on the "other" side of town.

On a Saturday when she knew the store would be busy, my mother cashed a couple of hundred dollars into one dollar bills and wadded them into her purse. She went into Woolworth's and walked around the aisles. The clerk started following her and my mother suddenly whipped around, jerked open her purse to show the money and loudly told the woman to get the hell off of her back or she'd buy the damn store and fire her.

The woman had treated her like trash, and she, in turn, had humiliated her.

Okay, you won't find this sort of advice in psychology books but . . . my mother used the only weapons she had. When reason and logic won't work, sometimes you have to cut the other person off at the knees.

3

Protecting Your Job

Corporations have no souls, but they can love each other.

—Henry Demarest Lloyd

We know more about how *to do* our job than *how to keep it*. And know little about what to do when we *lose it*. Every person who holds down a job should have some basic knowledge about their legal and intracompany rights, know how to protect their rights when they are terminated or injured, and have an "employment file" with critical documents in it.

The man in my office was fifty-nine years old. He was a middle-management employee earning a substantial wage. He was being terminated after twenty-four years with the company because his job function was no longer needed. His prospects of getting another job even remotely close to his former level were nil. The company was paying a high-priced consulting firm thousands of dollars to help him find another job, but the procedure was a cruel joke, conscience money, and the money would have been better spent as a bonus to him. At his age, the termination notice was a pink slip to his pride and sense of self-worth.

What antagonized me the most was the company's philosophy. When he hired on, it had been a small, family-oriented operation that emphasized loyalty of the company to the employees who returned the loyalty. When business was down, the company carried the slack at the expense of its bottom line for employees, who gave their best during the good times. The symbiotic relationship of one hand washing the other made the company a success so that the founders were able to merge the firm into a larger one and retire on their hard-earned fortunes.

But the success that the man in my office helped create came back to haunt him and others. The firm was no longer a "family." It was too big. Administrators with a computer chip for a heart were looking at the bottom line. A stroke here, a slash here, and their bottom line looked good. The fact that the pencil mark on an organizational chart might violate two decades of mutual trust and fidelity didn't mean a thing to the bean counter making the decision.

The concept of "job security" is gone because of the size and mobility of industries. New industries explode overnight—and others *implode*. Corporate conscience rests not in the hearts and minds of people but on the bottom line. One frightening "statistic" that goes far toward demonstrating how much we have lost in terms of the "family" concept of employment is "the phone company." During the darkest days of the Great Depression, the phone company prided itself on never laying off a single employee. Fifty years later, during the great communications boom of the eighties and nineties, phone companies terminated tens of thousands of jobs to make their profit margins even higher.

31

The only "sin" the man in my office had committed was being the same category as about 99 percent of the other employees in America: he was an "at will" employee.

Job Security Versus "At Will" Employment

In general, there are two types of employment status: at will and contractual.

"At will" refers to the fact that the employee keeps his/her job at the will of the employer. "Contractual" refers to agreements that relate to the employment (union agreements and civil service rules can involve contractual-type rights).

The general rule for "at will" employees is that, barring a discriminatory basis (such as age or sex) or other statutory basis (such as being wrongly fired for having to go on jury duty or being a whistle-blower), the company has a right to terminate your employment.

But even with "at will" employees, nonstatutory factors may come into play. Many companies, especially large ones, may have an employee manual that they give as much credence to as they do state and federal laws. Some courts have permitted employees to treat company policy manuals (sometimes even memos, bulletins, letters, verbal promises, unwritten policies, custom and practice in the industry and firm, even advertisements to solicit employees) as having much the same effect as a "contract" (a contract "implied" by the circumstances). Under most of these policy manuals and other manifestations of job security, firing can usually only be "for cause" and there are generally several steps involved. However, under all of them there will be a procedure for terminating employees in general for "economic" reasons.

Thus, while a company manual may give you certain rights, as long as they cross their t's and dot their i's, you are still an "at will" employee, and if they want to get rid of you, for cause if they have grounds, or just to make their bottom line look better, they will probably be able to do it. And unless you have a union to back you up, or a civil service–type procedure for protection, the chances of a person who is in the unemployment line having enough money to hire a lawyer to fight back are pretty bleak.

That is not to say that there haven't been people who had been treated heinously and had courageous lawyers behind them who walked out of courtrooms with multimillion-dollar judgments—but that happens about as often as people win the lottery.

The dilemma that the courts face is balancing the employer's right to hire and fire at will with the employee's right to be treated fairly and in good faith.

A written employment contract/agreement with the company is your best protection. Oral contracts are generally enforceable—and hell to prove. Few of us are in a bargaining position to get a "written contract" with a company, but if you are leaving Company A for a job at Company B, and Company B knows they are luring you away, you should ask for a confirmation letter describing your new position and send a CYA (Cover Your Ass) letter to the new employer. While these letters are far from job security, they are at least *something* to start building a case on. You'd be surprised how memories will fade when you've been on the new job three months and find yourself pink-slipped. (Make sure you don't let it appear you're trying to "document" things—companies don't like employees who know their rights and are willing to enforce them.)

Keeping Track of Your Rights in an Employment File

We all have a file at home for our bills. One for our savings and checking account. For our car, apartment or house, and old lottery tickets. None of those things are as important to us as our job, yet few people have a "job" file at home. They might have some papers at work, but they may not even be able to get to them when they come back from lunch and find the lock to their office has been changed and a pink slip has been nailed to the door (I'm being facetious, but I heard a story from a labor attorney, who swore to me that it was the gospel, that one of the big Silicon Valley companies planning the layoff of an entire division and worried that employees would pirate company secrets and equipment, held a fire drill—and when everyone was outside, the doors to the building were locked and the termination announcement made over loudspeakers).

Keep this caveat in mind when constructing an "employment" file: *Don't violate any company policy* in possessing or removing from the office any of the items I suggest you have in your file. A "no-no" is taking anything out of the office that the company does not authorize. You will probably find that almost everything you deal with at the company except the brand of paper clips is considered a trade secret, and you are not permitted to remove any of it from the office. When they are looking around for a reason to fire you, and you whip out or mention something that you are not supposed to have, you will have shot yourself in the foot.

- The Company Manual: Keep a copy of your company's policy manual at home. Keep the

34

old copies when the manual is replaced, especially the one you were hired under. As pointed out above, in some ways the "company manual" can be thought of as your bible of rights and benefits.

Don't just keep the manual—read it. *Know your rights*. But use some common sense about enforcing them. No one likes "jailhouse lawyers," and that's what your boss will see you as if you go around quoting the manual in your defense and advising others.

Knowing when to open your mouth is definitely the name of the game in terms of job security. When an employee calls me about a job threat, I ask them to bring in their copy of the company manual (again, making sure there is no rule about it leaving the office). Reading through it, we commonly find that the boss riding my client has not followed the manual's precise rules. Elated, the employee's instinct is to go to work the next day and make the boss eat the manual. *Wrong move*—if you believe you are about to be terminated, let the boss get right up to the point of terminating you, hopefully to the point of documenting it, and then file a grievance to get the dismissal overturned. Otherwise you have simply given the boss a chance to correct his/her error.

- Recruitment ad: If you respond to a recruitment ad, or if others in a like position did, keep a copy of the ad in your home employment file. It can come in handy if there is a later dispute over job description or benefits.
- Employee Bulletins: Many companies send out

bulletins periodically making announcements of changes in personnel policies and benefits. Keep a copy of these bulletins in your file.

- Personnel File: Some companies permit employees to have all or part of the contents of their personnel file. If you are so permitted, maintain a copy in your home, adding important documents like job reviews, commendations, and warnings.

- Diary: If you are having a problem at work, you should keep a "diary" of who-said-what-when-where-and-why. Remember, there is very little "right to privacy" on the job, and your supervisor may use some excuse to go through your desk while you are off for the day, so keep this at home. If there is any documentation that you can retain, such as a memo concerning the dispute, again, if you can do so without violating company policy, keep those in your file also.

- State Department of Unemployment/Human Resources Benefits Booklet: See the discussion below on why to get this booklet and how to plan strategy with it.

- Union/Civil Service Manual/Teacher Manual: If other manuals are available, such as one from your union, keep a copy of it in your file.

When Your Job Is on the Line

This section makes a significant presumption: that you want to keep your job and that there is something you can do to achieve that goal. If you are called out on a "fire-drill layoff" you obviously have no power to alter the situation. It's not unlike airplane crashes: There are survivable crashes (usually on takeoff or landing) and nonsurvivable crashes (like a midair collision). When you have a "survivable crash" at your place of employment, you have to be prepared to dodge the bullet.

Start with basics. Take out a piece of paper and define, in one paragraph, exactly what the problem is (you can do it—they start wars and make fifty-million-dollar movies off of one paragraph descriptions). Why a single paragraph? So you can focus. I am not asking you to write your life story or history of your grievances at the company—just define what the problem is.

Most people's inclination will be to write down that the problem is the supervisor doesn't like them or that there is a personality conflict. That may be true, but usually the abrasive relationship is a symptom of something related to job performance—either yours is not up to standards or the supervisor is being unrealistic. Go over the description with family, friends, your minister, a lawyer, anyone with some common sense. Refine it until it makes sense to you and you understand the situation. If you are the source of the problem (heaven forbid!), face up to it. If some one else is, try to define what is motivating the behavior.

"Empowerment" is a buzzword of the last couple of decades, and you empower yourself when you know what you are up against.

Next, define each of your alternatives (transferring, getting another job, early retirement, the poorhouse, etc.). And be realistic about the alternatives.

Then decide upon a course of action, again keeping your feet on the ground and head at a level of reality.

Put the plan into action.

But . . . have a backup position in case everything goes to

hell. If your decision is to find another job, and you can't afford loss in pay while you hunt, come up with a plan to find another job while you keep your present one. If your decision is to keep your job and deal with the problem, know what your next step will be when everything goes to hell.

If you decide to deal with the problem, don't ignore it: Get your supervisor to work with you by demonstrating your willingness to meet his/her standards.

What don't you want to do? Ignore the problem. You just give others the opportunity to gut you.

Don't make an emotional response to the problem. Stress from work, stress from home and brought to work can cause you to *break down* or *strike back* when the company starts putting the screws to you. Both responses are inappropriate and create the opportunity for others to victimize you.

Knowing how to negotiate will help us stand up for our rights . . . but remember we may be in a no-win situation. On my first job, a coworker said, "Remember, kid, when the boss is right, he's right—when the boss is wrong, he's right." If you've got a couple of kids, a mortgage, and a few gray hairs, the better part of valor may be to grin and bear the abuse in the hopes that he or she gets transferred, promoted, or has a café coronary from a tough piece of meat in the company cafeteria.

I became an attorney twenty-some years ago, and when I hired my first secretary, I bought her a book on the duties of a legal secretary. We howled with laughter over one section that lectured the secretary on his/her duties, giving a laundry list of problems you were supposed to overcome and still get to work on time (flat tires, your kid's flu, etc.). One of the statements was to the effect that if you found out that morning your mother had cancer, you were still supposed to perform your duties with a smile on your face no matter what you felt in your heart . . .

That statement has more meaning today than it did two decades ago. Corporations today can be astonishingly cold about our personal problems. Everyone is worried about their own job. No matter what a great employee we have been in the past, or what relationship we have had with our superiors, a "family" or "personal" crises that extends into weeks or months, or different crises that keep popping up, is going to wear thin very fast.

While our boss nods sympathetically as we sob about our problems (and the problems may be very real and very serious), or sits passively while we pound on him or her because we are the type to project our stress with anger, what may be going on in the supervisor's mind is the thought of letting us go before we contaminate his or her job—not to mention that we will be the topic of discussion at lunch and shortly thereafter everyone in the company will know our life story. (Remember that old saying, "Familiarity breeds contempt." Letting others know that we're going through a messy divorce, our kid's in jail for burglarizing the neighbor's house to feed his drug problem, or we are suffering midlife meltdown, is a quick way to breed contempt—it doesn't matter that *their* kids are crack addicts and they're in their third divorce, they still feel superior because it's our dirty laundry being aired.)

If we have a "work file" that lays out our rights and duties, and copies of past evaluations, we will have a frame of reference to work from in dealing with the problem and perhaps even materials to demonstrate our position.

If you are a member of a union or other organization that provides legal advice or information when you are in trouble, and you have a problem at work, reach for the advice or other support materials at the first sign of trouble. If that type of support is not available, talk to your minister, spend a couple hundred dollars and see a lawyer, and/or throw the problem and alternatives out on the table with friends and let them play devil's advocate. Talking to others will help you see the forest from the trees and focus on the real issues.

Besides advising many people and companies on work problems, I've run my own business, worked for mama-papa companies, and held a management job with one of the corporate giants. My experiences have led me to conclude that while individuals in large companies may be decent, the companies themselves cannot be depended upon because *everyone is expendable.* Management changes. The "rules" change. There is no job security. You have to protect yourself. The Japanese say business is war. Americans say war is hell. Surviving at work is sometimes hell and war.

Unemployment Benefits

Unemployment claims are a potential snake pit. General rules concerning qualifying for benefits are laid out below but state laws vary, and while you can use the materials below as a guide, you have to check precise requirements in your locale.

In most states you cannot collect unemployment benefits, or are severely penalized, if you *quit* your job as opposed to being *terminated* by your employer.

This is an area where pride goes before a fall: Walking off the job in a huff may mean the difference between surviving financially until you find another job or sticking up liquor stores.

A basic rule for dealing with the unemployment office is

to *know what the rules are* before committing hari-kari filling out an application for benefits. You are going to have to give a reason for leaving your past employment. The reason you place on the application has to correspond to the permissible reasons listed in the unemployment benefit regulations. Those reasons are typically outlined in a booklet available at the unemployment office or sometimes can be ascertained by a telephone call.

Do not put down a false reason. The company you left will be sent a form to fill out and will put down their version as to why you left.

In most states you are eligible for unemployment if you have been laid off or you quit for "good cause." By "laid off" I am referring to a company-initiated termination which may have come about because the company is cutting back, is eliminating the job title, or for any number of reasons (other than the "misconduct" mentioned below), just doesn't want you working there anymore. "Quitting" refers to the termination being initiated by you. If you quit your job, your eligibility for unemployment benefits will depend upon the reason (you generally qualify for benefits if you quit for "good cause").

What is a good cause? Sometimes it's a judgment call by the person interviewing you to determine eligibility and sometimes it's etched in stone. If you leave work when asked by the employer to resign or face being fired or forced to take a leave of absence, that is generally good cause (unless the underlying reason for being fired involves misconduct).

Leaving work due to mere dislike, distaste, or minor inconvenience caused by working conditions is generally not good cause.

Leaving because of sexual harassment, being subjected to verbal or physical abuse, discrimination, and threats involving health, safety, or mental well-being are all good cause. Of course, being able to prove the good cause is likely to be a major problem.

Being discharged for "misconduct" usually results in a denial of benefits, but you can fight it. Some employers falsely report that an employee left for "misconduct" in hopes of cheating the employee out of unemployment benefits. True misconduct is generally held to be willful and wanton disregard of the employer's interests to the point where the employee's actions appear deliberate or negligent to the point of culpability. Actions such as repeated inexcusable tardiness, drinking, drugs, dishonesty, insubordination, gross negligence, and use of vulgar, abusive, offensive, or obscene language are examples of potential "misconduct."

Inefficiency, unsatisfactory conduct, inadvertence, ordinary negligence, or good-faith errors in judgment are not generally "misconduct" and generally do not result in a denial of benefits.

Before you quit, get fired, or laid off, make a trip to the unemployment office and get a copy of an *unemployment-benefits booklet*.

Read it.

Understand what will qualify you for benefits and how much you will receive.

Know what actions at work will disqualify you from benefits.

Know how to answer the questions posed by an unemployment interviewer before the questions are asked. One of my clients was not available for work one day because she stayed home to take care of her sick daughter. She was naive enough to tell the interviewer that she had stayed home to care for the little girl. It cost her the benefit check for the week.

Benefits vary from state to state but are generally in the

neighborhood of half to two-thirds of your weekly pay for a designated period in the past—and up to a maximum amount. They make sure you don't get enough money to really enjoy being out of work—the schedule of benefits is designed to help you limp along at the starvation level for a few months while you're finding another job.

Wrongful Termination and Tort Remedies

During the 1980s lawyers won a series of victories against corporate America on behalf of employees who had been wronged by their employers. Within a few years appellate courts were toning down the victories. Grievous wrongs are probably still actionable, but it is harder to win and often the potential recoveries are less. However, once in a while a jury still gets outraged at hearing how a company ripped the heart from an employee and makes the company pay.

A "wrongful-termination" lawsuit may arise from a breach of an express or implied employment contract or from a combination of various contract and tort theories (torts are legal wrongs for which civil remedies may be available and include offenses such as infliction of emotional distress, fraud, battery, defamation, and invasion of privacy). What constitutes an actionable case varies from state to state.

Issues that lawyers and courts are going to be interested in are whether the employee was treated fairly and in good faith—and if not treated fairly, was the employer's conduct something that is actionable at law (and from the lawyer and clients point of view, financially worth pursuing).

These are expensive cases to litigate and tough cases to win. Don't quit your day job because you're expecting to hit the jackpot with a lawsuit against your employer.

Workers Compensation Rights

This statutory scheme applies to on-the-job injuries (physical injuries and emotional trauma such as stress).

Basically, in most states the legislature has taken away the employees' right to sue the employer for a work-related injury in return for the employees getting "no fault" workers compensation benefits. In general, it does not matter how the injury came about (i.e., whether a fellow employee was negligent or you were just plain stupid), you are usually still entitled to benefits.

Like any other rule there are many exceptions: For example, if a fellow employee punched you in the nose, you may by able to sue the employee in a law court for battery and obtain workers compensation benefits from your employer in a workers compensation court. If you get injured on the job as a result of a ladder breaking, you may be able to sue the ladder manufacturer in a law court and get workers compensation benefits from your employer.

Most "comp claims" are handled between you and your employer's comp insurance company without the help of a lawyer. You should contact a lawyer (or other authorized claimant's representative) for any significant injury. Because comp benefits are typically low and much of the system is automatic, this is not an area where you can expect to get a great deal of attention from a lawyer because attorney fees are very low. Typically, these cases are handled by lawyers who might be handling ten times more files than other types of lawyers and they have little time to hold your hand during the procedure (because the lawyers handle huge volumes of cases and make little money on each case, they are among the worst lawyers to return clients' phone calls).

Americans with Disabilities

The ADA (Americans With Disabilities Act) is one of the more powerful tools against discrimination. The act basically applies to a person who has a physical or mental impairment that substantially limits one or more major life activities. ("Impairment" is broadly interpreted to include such conditions as defects in vision, problems with walking, hearing, speaking, bodily motor impairments, and the like). Persons with temporary problems and minor problems are generally not covered by the act. Under certain circumstances, AIDS is a covered condition. Coverage of alcohol- and drug-abuse conditions is a complex problem. While current usage may not be covered, there are situations in which long-term prior use may have created a covered disability.

In general, the act applies to all but the smallest employers and businesses.

The act has a two-pronged effect: It provides a standard for "accommodating" persons with disabilities in terms of shopping, schooling, etc., and it provides "employment" standards for the disabled.

Its "accommodation" requirements deal with curbs, ramps, store aisles, accessibility to merchandise, parking, rest rooms, and the like.

The act's "employment" provisions prohibit discrimination against qualified individuals based upon disability. The discrimination can be in the form of recruiting, hiring, terms and conditions of employment, or any other aspect that results is discrimination.

Discrimination

This is a complex subject, and while I can give you tips on some of your rights, there are so many variables, ranging from size and type of company to where you live, that specifics are hard to pin down.

The following are some of the general areas of discrimination:

- Age: Companies cannot discriminate against applicants and employees over forty years old. If you believe age will be a problem in getting a job, don't put your age on your résumé. Nor should you put down dates (such as year you graduated from high school or college) from which your approximate age can be calculated. A requirement that you state your age during an interview or on an application generally violates the law.
- Race, Color and National Origin: Discrimination on any of these bases is obviously unlawful, but employers desiring to discriminate by excluding a particular racial group from their hiring have come up with an incredible number of different criteria to pull this off. For example, refusing to hire based upon such things as previous arrests may be reasonably based—or may camouflage discrimination because some minorities qualified for the job may simply have a higher incident of arrests, military problems, or poor credit status, and the situation may not have any reasonable relationship to job qualification.

- Sex: Discrimination in this area can also be blatant or subtle. Employers with discriminatory policies sometimes use innocent-sounding questions (about place of birth, maiden name, photographs, organizational membership) to get information that they can use to discriminate with.

  There may even be "height" and "weight" discriminatory policies if the requirements are not reasonably related to the job performance (typically, theses type of requirements have been used to discriminate against women and minorities).

  Questions about marital status, pregnancy, future child-bearing plans, how many children are in the household, the ages of children, are also used to discriminate. These questions are proper when they are related to postemployment tax and insurance information. It is a violation of federal law to have different policies for the hiring of men and women with preschool as opposed to older children.

- Religion: In general, employers cannot discriminate over religious affiliations. Like any other rule, the exceptions take a big bite out of the rule. Religious organizations and schools affiliated with a religious group are exempt, not to mention that only "reasonable efforts" are generally required by an employer to accommodate an employee's work schedule that conflicts with the employee's religious belief (for example, working on Saturdays or Sundays, depending on belief).

There are also a number of miscellaneous state and federal statutes that may in general protect employees (governing discharge for union activities, health and safety on the job, whistle-blowers, retirement/pension rights and vesting, wages, overtime, working conditions, underage workers, jury duty, military service, pregnancy, and many more subjects).

As pointed out, there are exceptions and variations to every one of the rules, and the only way you are going to be able to get a viable opinion on your rights is to contact the state and federal regulatory agencies (such as the EEOC, OSHA, and state labor boards), a union attorney, or an otherwise knowledgeable labor-law attorney.

State Labor Department

Most states have a regulatory agency that goes to bat for the employee in disputes involving wages, overtime, working hours, and conditions. The agencies usually will not get involved in contractual disputes and wrongful termination. Most of the cases involve employees making claims for wages left unpaid after they left the job or for overtime pay not paid during their employment.

While I don't discourage you from seeking help from a labor board, this is another one of those "don't quit your day job" scenarios—these agencies are typically slow, bureaucratic, overwhelmed with cases, and often impotent in terms of what they can actually do to an employer. My experience has been that (1) the agencies are better in theory than practice, (2) many of the grievances put before it are grudge matches between a former employee and the owner or manager of the place of employment

Once in a while justice happens. I represented a group of laborers who had been cheated out of thousands of dollars in legally mandated overtime pay, and it felt good to put the screws to the employers who had put the screws to them.

4

Relationships and Divorce

If I can stop one Heart from breaking
I shall not live in Vain
If I can ease one Life the Aching
Or cool one Pain
Or help one fainting Robin
Unto his Nest again
I shall not live in Vain.

—Emily Dickinson

We are human and even the best of us will have ups and downs and the good and the bad in relationships and marriage. It's inevitable that sometimes our emotions will be shredded and our hearts ripped. But we have to maintain control and responsibility for our own lives regardless of the pain. When we lose control of our emotions, we turn our lives over to lawyers, counselors, and courts to tell us how we are supposed to feel and dictate how we are to raise our children. When that happens, we have victimized ourselves financially and emotionally and give others the opportunity to take advantage of us.

Early in my career, I handled many divorces because it was the most common "legal" problem people had, it paid the rent, and I believed it offered an opportunity to help people. In later years I still did one occasionally if it was a significant case, and I was certain that it was not going to be an emotional bomb. In doing divorces, I represented some very intelligent, wonderfully rational and reasonable people who did their best to make the difficult process of dealing with the trauma of having lawyers, counselors, and courts invading their privacy as little damaging as possible to their spouse and children. I also represented people who turned the process into horrors that even Stephen King couldn't imagine—when love turned to hate, emotions were shredded, children got ripped to pieces in custody battles, and blood was spilled over possession of spoons and the family parakeet. Just as bad was the *pathos*, listening to women and men break down and tell me of love never fulfilled.

I sucked in the problems of my clients like an emotional leech, feeling their pain and losses. I couldn't stand the idea of the "wrong" parent (i.e., the person I didn't represent) getting custody of children. I woke up in the middle of the night agonizing over the cases and rehearsing the next day's court proceedings in my mind so I could anticipate every move the other side might make and lay traps to take them by surprise. It made me effective in court, but the trauma depressed me, and I began to dread the emotionally charged cases—and I was only experiencing the pain *vicariously*. My poor client was the one suffering the real wounds. Sometimes the wounds were self-inflicted.

There's an old Italian proverb that a lawsuit is a tree in a lawyer's garden and some attorneys get a whole orchard from a divorce. They consider a divorce a billing cow, and if the parties lost their cool and began to get petty or mean with each other, it only meant that the cow was giving more milk. One morning I got a call from an attorney that sounded like a whole truckload of milk was on the way.

"Your client has molested his daughter," he told me.

Child molesters come in all shapes and sizes, but they generally fit a profile, and my client wasn't anywhere in the equation. And this was not the first time I had heard the allegation in a divorce setting.

Boiled down to basics, what happened was this: Husband and wife are getting a divorce. Husband has a new girlfriend. New girlfriend meets husband's young daughter on daughter's weekend visit with husband. Shortly thereafter new girlfriend sends daughter a gift on her birthday. Wife calls her lawyer and says husband has molested daughter.

There is also a male counterpart to the scenario: Husband, during course of divorce, finds out wife has a new boyfriend. Husband calls his attorney and says that his wife and new boyfriend had sex on the living-room couch in front of the husband's young children.

I'm not telling you that some men don't molest their children and some women don't have sex in front of children—if the average person spent a couple of hours in a child dependency courtroom listening to the horrors that parents do to children, they would come away sorely questioning the human spirit. But like other lawyers, I've heard these "molestation" and "public-sex" allegations many times in divorces, and even though they always require an investigation, I can't remember a single incident where there was anything but spite behind the stories. As you might expect, the charge is usually made *after* the parties separate and when a custody battle or some other factor comes into play.

When a wife and husband abandon all sense of reason-ableness and hide behind their lawyers to throw salvos at each other, the courts will ultimately have to issue orders in-structing the two as to (1) which parent has physical cus-tody of children, (2) which parent had "legal" custody (i.e., for example, to sign for medical treatment), (3) when the parent who does not have custody may visit the child, (4) whether the visitation is to be supervised or unsupervised, (5) the lifestyle the child would have (as determined by child support), (6) whether the child would go to public or pri-vate schools, (7) who will have the child on birthdays, holi-days, and school vacations, (8) and limitations on taking the child across a state line.

This order was not designed for a case in which there was a molestation allegation—*these are standard terms in al-most all custody cases.* This is not an order the court puts out to "bad" people—these are the standard terms used for the divorces of doctors, lawyers, movie stars, CEOs, gold-medal Olympians, and the checker at the supermarket.

When two successful, intelligent people turn their divorce into an emotional bloodbath, they lose control. Lawyers, counselors, CPAs, and the courts take over their lives, each ripping off a piece to handle.

And children become the biggest victim of all. Besides the damage to the child's emotions, their relationship with their parents is now dictated by strangers.

Divorces are just one facet of relationships in which people make victims of themselves and others. I've dealt with thousands of "relationship" problems in a wide vari-ety of contexts and mentally cataloged some of the most common problems into what I call the "deadly sins of rela-tionships." While these interpersonal situations seem like psychological problems, we don't suffer in a vacuum, and the problems can cost us money and careers.

Sometimes they even put us in jail.

The first sin is *not being able to let go*. In a manner of speaking, this sin makes a monkey out of us. . . .

I sat in court and watched a psychiatrist being questioned about my client, a prominent businessman who was on trial for shooting his wife. The couple had been going through a divorce after over twenty years of marriage. It had been a rough couple of decades for them, beating on each other, police being called to their home on occasion, until he shot her. It was only a minor wound, but the law takes a dim view of a spouse who shoots the other spouse.

The psychiatrist was explaining for the jury the character flaw that drove my client to shoot his wife. He described it as the "obsessional" conduct of a person who can't "let go" and told the story of how monkeys are trapped in Indonesia.

Monkey hunters cut the top out of a coconut and drain the juice. They nail the coconut shell to a tree trunk and fill it with nuts. Monkeys are attracted to the shell by the smell of the nuts, and when one reaches in and grabs a handful of nuts, it can't get its hand out because it won't let go of the nuts. It will stay trapped until the hunters return.

I don't pretend to know anything about monkeys and coconuts, but I have dealt with a lot of people who don't know when to let go. I've represented them in criminal courts after they harmed someone they love. I've represented them in divorce court and watched them sacrifice everything, even their children, to get back at their spouse. I've represented businesspeople who held on until they went under. And I've felt the hurt of good, hardworking people who drove their financial dreams into nightmares or were victimized emotionally, psychologically, sometimes violently, by someone who wouldn't let go of them.

Not being able to let go is related to the next sin: *making others responsible for our happiness.* The problem with making others responsible for our happiness is that nothing is permanent in this world—not relationships, not marriages, and certainly not even life itself. No matter how much we love someone, no matter how much we love each other, we cannot rely on them being in our lives forever. That does not meant that we are not to love deeply and with all of our heart and soul or that the loss of a loved one for whatever reason will not devastate us, but it does mean we need to have some *independent basis for happiness.* What that basis will be will depend upon our own desires and personalities, but the need is there for each of us to fill ourselves with *something* besides the essence of the one we love.

Just as we can't let someone take charge of our emotional security, we shouldn't fall into the trap of letting someone else be responsible for our *financial security.* I've seen this most often in divorces.

Disabuse yourself of any notion that modern community-property laws compensate the homemaker equally with the wage-earner. Such laws divide the value of property at the time of the split, including the business or profession of the higher-earning spouse, and at that time it is an equal division. But there is no way that the law can compensate a loving, devoted spouse for decades of self-sacrifice that has left them less able to provide themselves with the same quality of life as the spouse who has spent the time building a career.

Another problem is not realizing that *we don't choose whom we love.*

I listened to two people at a party, a psychologist and a young woman, have a lengthy discussion about the young woman's problems with her estranged boyfriend, who has a drug problem. The young woman is attractive, intelligent, hardworking, and ambitious. She had a child with the problem boyfriend, and she is raising the child as a single mom. The boyfriend is just the opposite—unable to keep a job, he mooches off of his parents and occasionally drops into the young woman's life just long enough for her emotions to get raked raw.

At one point the psychologist said to her, "We know what's wrong with the boyfriend, but you have to come to grips with what's wrong with *you* for letting this problem back in your life over and over." The young woman had been agonizing over whether something was wrong with her because she kept opening the door to the boyfriend, so the comment struck home.

I didn't agree with the psychologist's interpretation that there was something "wrong" with the young woman. My experience in dealing with people, often at their worst and with their emotions exposed, often ripping each other to pieces, sometimes mentally, frequently violently, is that *we don't choose whom we love*. Good women love bad men and good men love bad women not because they have a mental defect that they can cure with a definition out of a psychology book but because of a mysterious process we call "chemistry."

Listening to people trying to describe their emotional response to someone they were divorcing or breaking up with, I discovered that frequently they were saying the same thing: They still loved the person—*but couldn't stand to be around them*. The sensual attraction was there but compatibility wasn't.

The young woman fell in love with someone whose lifestyle grated on her like fingernails scraping on a chalkboard. There was nothing she could do about falling in love with the wrong person. But there was plenty she could do about dealing with the person and how we deal with it directly relates to victimization.

Beating on ourselves, as the young woman was doing, or beating on the other person, which is how many people react, makes victims out of us and them. The solution is not to project blame or suck it in but to understand that we didn't choose this person to love but we can choose how we will respond to the pain. And then make the appropriate responses.

Loving too much is another way we make ourselves victims.

Dealing with marriages and relationships, I came to the conclusion that there were two types of people in relationships: those who were emotionally interactive, people who need to give and get back reinforcement about love, who need to touch and feel the relationship, and those who were emotionally independent. A person who wishes to interact and interrelate gives more emotionally to a relationship and needs more back.

A typical scenario was that a woman would come into my office and tell me she wanted a divorce. The marriage was most often five years old or less and there usually was a child involved. There is a need for people in these situations to bare their souls, and what I heard most often was that the two people simply had different interests. Frequently the wife had the more sensitive nature, while the husband's notion of sensitivity was golf outings and watching football.

In talking to people, listening to why love had turned cold, or just as often had turned bitter and angry, I found essentially that most of the people were mismatched. What occurred was that a person who was emotionally interactive had teamed up with a person who was emotionally independent.

When two emotionally interactive people married, the marriage worked.

When two emotionally independent people got together, the marriage worked.

When the two were mixed, the chemistry was more volatile.

Fear of the unknown is another relationship sin. Usually the "unknown" that is feared is being left alone. Some of us hang on to a relationship as a crutch because we don't believe that we will find anyone else to love us.

If there is anything I've learned about human nature, it is that if we've found one person to love us, there will be someone else in this world for us if the need arises. It all goes back to chemistry. If we go out and circulate, we'll eventually find someone we click with just like we found the last one. Sound too simple? *It is simple.* We complicate it out of fear of losing what we have and fear of rejection from someone new. It isn't that hard to find companionship in this world if you are willing to give it an *effort.* Marriages and relationships are hard work. If we want a successful one, we have to put in the work.

The last sin is the culmination of all the others: *turning love into hate.* There is no area in which we make ourselves more often a victim than when love goes sour and our emotions get out of control. And there are no situations in which we are emotionally scarred more often.

We're human, and we can get hurt. Sometimes we strike back when we're hurt. But when we lose control and abandon our responsibilities to keep a rein on our emotions, we hurt ourselves and others.

All of us in one way or another sometimes find ourselves victims of those we love. Parents feed the destructive habits of their children by running interference for them rather than making them take charge of their own lives, spouses use guilt and financial pressures to emotionally cripple each other—and their children.

This is the area where most of the emotional scars from divorces get carved onto us, our spouse, and children. Hell breaks loose and rationality melts down when we lose control of our emotions. When that happens, it inevitably comes back to bite us. In a relationship, we give the other person the opportunity to write us off as irrational. In a divorce, we stimulate an array of negative reactions: We turn off our own lawyer, we give the other lawyer and our spouse the opportunity to victimize us because word of our conduct will alienate the judge and marriage counselors assigned to our case. Those negative "vibes" will affect us in how property is distributed and custody and visitation rights are assigned. And we inadvertently hurt our children.

That is not to say you shouldn't absolutely stand up for your rights to keep your spouse from taking advantage of you. But when you fight back with an outburst of emotions, you are tying one hand behind you because you are not going to focus on the real problems, make rational decisions, keep from paying your lawyer through the nose, and get the sympathy of the judge who has heard as much emotional trauma as any human being could stand and now shuts him/herself off from it.

There are few divorces and relationship meltdowns in which there isn't recrimination. There is going to be emotional pain and scars. The objective is to reduce the emotional damage and, if not to come out a winner, to make sure it is at least a draw. (I have to admit that an occasional act of vindictiveness deserves credit just for the ingenuity of it—in one case, a wife who suspected her clotheshorse husband of cheating cut the crotch out of his suits—all twenty of them!)

Life is not fair. People get married and promise to be together forever, and "forever" currently averages less than five years.

There is no way that the disintegration of a relationship or a marriage is not going to hurt. But we have to keep from having the trauma destroy us and our children.

When the reaction, the *very human* reaction, is to strike out, we make a victim of ourselves by giving our spouse, lawyers, and the courts opportunities to make victims of us. And we make victims of the innocent children involved.

I had a movie director tell me that he learned more from studying a film that flopped than a really good one because *what not to do* stands out so well. The same can be true of people. We can often find solutions to our own problems by asking ourselves where others went wrong. Sometimes these people are highly successful in one area—a career for example—and fail in another—as in a relationship or as a parent.

Some of them have such unfulfilled potential or unsatisfied yearnings for love that I want to tell them they need a wake-up call about their people skills. Some of these people are friends and family.

Sometimes the person needing the wake-up call is oneself.

It's impossible to go through life without judging others, but when it comes to marriage and relationships, we need to avoid judgments because we never really know the whispers and secrets that have passed behind the bedroom door.

In my case I felt the undercurrent of bitterness that my mother had toward my father, and I never knew during their lives what had caused it. I had just assumed that it arose from her reaction to his temper and drinking and I was an adult myself before I was told that the bitterness had arisen from a moment of darkness. My mother never spoke to me about it, but she conveyed her pain in a different way:

I was never allowed to own anything yellow. When I was a kid and wanted to buy a yellow shirt, she told me I couldn't have it, that yellow was the color of death.

It was after my mother's death, during a family gathering, that my older sister told me the story behind my mother's fear of letting me wear yellow.

I had an older brother, Victor, whom I was too young to remember. When Victor was seven years old my father slapped Victor, and he left the house crying. A little later neighborhood children came running and told my mother that Victor had fallen into the creek behind our house. When my mother reached the creek Victor was underwater and what froze in her mind was the blur of the yellow shirt he was wearing. He was dead when she pulled him out of the water.

My parents have been dead many years but I can still remember my mother telling my father that she knew she would die before him, and, when she did, she'd pull him into the grave with her. My mother did die first, and my father passed unexpectedly two days later.

Some things in life cannot be forgotten or forgiven, and it is not for us to judge the pain of others. We may have a clue as to the source of hurt between two people, but we don't know what passed between them that was the source of the love that brought them together in the first place.

A great American, Eleanor Roosevelt, in her book, *You Learn by Living,* gave advice that can guide us whether we are involved in a difficult relationship or any other life crisis.

"You gain strength, courage and confidence by every experience in which you really stop to look fear in the face. You are able to say to yourself, 'I have lived through this horror. I can take the next thing that comes along.' . . . You must do the thing you think you cannot do."

And as her husband, President Franklin Delano Roosevelt, said when we faced the greatest crisis in American history, *"The only thing we have to fear is fear itself."*

5

Credit Cards, Creditors, and Rip-offs

Money doesn't talk, it swears.

—Bob Dylan

High limits on credit cards have made us slaves to the banks. We would be outraged if a mugger took a thousand dollars from us on a street corner, but most of us pay more than that each year to lending institutions who steal with a pen. Getting control of credit is a matter of planning and budgeting. When control is lost, there are ways to negotiate payments and interest reductions. When all else fails, there are several forms of bankruptcy. A new "credit crime" that is becoming epidemic is "stolen identity," where thieves actually use our credit information to obtain credit themselves and leave us holding the bag.

Ever hear about someone stealing another person's identity? Don't think it can't happen—it happened to my associate. My associate is a Beverly Hills lawyer (I know, you lost sympathy already, but hang on because this guy and his wife worked hard for everything they have and this could happen to you or anyone else). A thief gained access to his personal information (name, address, social security number, perhaps even credit-card numbers).

The information was most likely gained by someone who was able to tap into his credit record or an application for credit. Candidates for the thief might be someone working where my associate banked, a credit-card company, a mortgage company, or perhaps someone working at a credit-reporting agency. The way our credit records (which for most of us are literally our whole financial history) are spread around in computers and companies, it is not difficult to gain private information. In other words, many thousands of people had access to his credit information by just tapping into the computer on their desk. Out of those thousands of potential thieves, there was at least one real thief who made my associate's life hell.

Using the private information, the thief first had a number of credit cards issued in my associate's name but sent to vacant apartments and houses in a low-income neighborhood where the thief had access to the porches and mailboxes. After obtaining the credit cards, the thief went on a shopping spree, ordering dozens of pairs of expensive tennis shoes, jewelry, and other easy-resale items—almost always by telephone and with the goods delivered to the vacant locations.

The scam went on and on, with the thief moving the drop point from one vacant dwelling to another and applying for more cards as my associate canceled cards. One credit-card company kept issuing cards to the thief over and over again—*six* cards in all, five of them issued after my associate warned them that the cards were being applied for fraudulently.

The thief was never caught and after a few months he or she crawled back into the woodwork, but it left my associate with a continuous headache for over a year (probably serves him right for having such a good credit rating).

Bear in mind that my associate never did anything wrong. He did not give out information to a thief—he gave it to his bank or in applying for a mortgage or in some other manner, and the thief accessed the file.

Major credit-reporting agencies get hundreds of thousands of calls a year concerning credit-card fraud, and a growing number of the calls concern "identity theft" in which a thief has grabbed a lost or stolen card and does not go on a brief shopping spree but actually applies for credit using another person's personal information.

If the crime happens to you, do everything you can to protect your credit, and report the matter not just to the local police, but to the FBI and Postal Inspectors.

There is not much you are able to do about someone accessing your credit file at your bank or mortgage company, but too many people do have problems because they have made themselves a victim by inadvertently giving information to a thief.

This commonly happens when you discard "preapproved" credit notices in your trash without tearing them up, giving out information to store clerks (such as your address and telephone number) when they already have the imprint of your card because you are making a purchase, giving information such as your social security number over the telephone to scam callers, and failing to destroy the excess sheets in credit slips that contain your account number.

And you can help the cause against credit fraud by reducing the number of cards you carry around in your wallet or purse, which are thus subject to loss and misuse.

If the average person opened their wallet or purse, it

would not be unusual to find they possess bank-type credit cards, an ATM card, gas cards, department-store cards, a phone card, health-plan card, and social security card, along with a driver's license, money, and the rest of their life story.

Now ask yourself if you really need to carry all of the credit cards you haul around. I did this before taking a trip recently and while it was painful, I found that I really did not need most of the cards for my survival. The cards are too much of a security blanket for me to cancel (hell, I'd have to pay them off before I could cancel them), but I did remove all but the few I really needed on a daily basis for an emergency (plus one more in case of an *emergency*-emergency).

The point is not to carry your whole financial life around in your wallet. As I mention in the section on traveling, my wife had that habit, and it caused a lot of misery when she had her purse stolen and we had to figure out how to cancel a couple dozen cards when we were three thousand miles from home.

Over the years I have received solicitations from outfits that register all of your cards and, in case of loss, notifies the issuers of all the cards with just one phone call from me. I didn't have that service and sorely wished I did that night. But did I sign up for it afterward? I have to admit I didn't. What we have done instead is clean out our wallets so we only carry the cards we use regularly and have put away the cards we use occasionally.

I know my social security number, but if you do not know yours, I suggest rather than carrying the card, write it on a slip of paper in your wallet. You might even devise a code for scrambling the numbers so if you lose your wallet, the thief won't get your number (social security numbers are often used on medical cards, so you may be carrying around the number anyway).

I don't carry a phone card, but have scrambled the number in my wallet. (Don't forget that you have to figure out how to *unscramble* the number when you need it, so don't get too clever.)

In addition, we have prepared a list of our cards with the following information:

- The issuer.
- Account number.
- Lost or stolen notification number.

I put the list in a sealed envelope and gave it to a close relative to hold. Hopefully she will remember where she put the list when we call from Timbuktu and tell her we need to notify our credit-card companies because a camel ate my wallet.

A couple of tips on notifying credit-card companies about losses:

Do it immediately upon discovery, no matter where you are. While doing last-minute shopping on Christmas Eve, my wife discovered at eleven o'clock in the morning that she had lost a credit card earlier—when she called in the loss a couple of hours later the card had already been used—repeatedly.

When you call the loss in, note the date, time, and name of the person at the credit-card company who takes the call in case the issue comes up later as to whether you reported the loss. Most credit-card companies have representatives on duty twenty-four hours a day to take loss reports.

Or, you might just consider signing up with one of the notification services.

There are scams in which persons claiming to be representatives of credit-card companies call to "verify" personal information. Unless you have initiated the call to the company yourself, I would not give out personal information to anyone.

You have to concern yourself about using credit cards over the Internet. While the vast majority of Internet businesses are legitimate, there are rotten apples as in any endeavor. Just make sure the entity you are dealing with is a legitimate business. And before placing an order, make sure you see the "security" system information on the screen that tells you others cannot access your information on their system.

Telephone credit cards are another troublesome problem. There have been a number of instances where crooks hang around pay telephones where credit cards are frequently used (like airports and train stations) and jot down your number as they watch you use it. There is not much you can do about this except fight with the long-distance carrier after you get the bill for fraudulent calls. You would look a little funny huddling close to the telephone and staring about suspiciously as if you are surrounded by Ali Baba and the Forty Thieves.

Dealing with Credit Meltdown

To err is human and many of us are more *human* than others. In the days Before Plastic people lived off of their paychecks and put a little aside each week for a rainy day. Most of us lack that rainy-day trait because everything has become automatic. Just as most of us lost the skill to mentally add up a column of figures and became dependent on calculators to do our math for us, we have left much of our financial planning to automatic withdrawals from our pay-checks. When we gave up control of our financial planning, we gave up responsibility for our day-to-day activities. Along came easy credit, and we got into the habit of using plastic. Once they had us hooked on plastic they raised the roof on credit lines so we could go deeper and deeper into debt.

How we got there is less important than what to do when we get over our heads in credit from bad decisions, failure to budget, loss of a job, divorce (probably the major cause of credit disasters in America), or illness. A number of people are forced into personal bankruptcy from the failure of a small business and a surprising number from having gone under helping a spouse or friend. I had one young woman consult me who had gone deep into credit-card debt raising money to keep her sister's business going until the business finally went under.

Getting a handle on dealing with creditors and credit meltdown requires essentially the same skills as dealing with dividing property in a divorce—you need to do an accounting to see where you stand. You need to know what you owe, what you have coming in and what you have going out. The other equation is budgeting to squeeze more out of your income to apply to your creditors.

If you cannot physically or mentally deal with the problem of getting your income and credit into line, look in the yellow pages for a firm that helps with personal budgeting. If you live in a community where these services are not available, consult an accountant or bookkeeper.

While this may sound "basic," the fact is that most of the people who consult lawyers about personal financial problems and bankruptcy walk into their office dazed with a bag full of papers and expect the lawyer to add up the figures and tell them where they stand financially.

Assuming that after the figures are added up you find the situation is hopeless, and you cannot meet your bills even with planning, budgeting, and bill consolidations, you have two choices: to attempt to negotiate a "settlement" of your debts or bankruptcy.

Credit-card companies in the past would not give people any slack at all in reducing payments or interest, but today in an age where bankruptcies are skyrocketing, there is much more willingness to cut a deal with a debtor who wants to pay but needs a helping hand. You get the process rolling by figuring out what you can pay your creditors and then contacting the creditor on its 800 number. Explain the problem to the representative, and you will usually be referred to a special group that handles these reduced-payment requests. If that does not work, send a letter explaining the problem and ask to be contacted by a credit manager.

What should you shoot for with this procedure? A reduction in the interest rate and/or a reduction in the monthly payments. You end up paying longer, but have some breathing space in which to make the payments.

This assumes that you are willing and able to deal with a payment plan. Will it ruin your credit? Probably . . . while you have done the decent thing and deserve applause for riding out the storm, the "computer program" that rates your credit standing is probably going to give you a black mark.

Most people are more fatalistic about their situation and rather than working out a reduced payment plan they simply get rid of the debts in bankruptcy.

Bankruptcy is a fundamental right of all Americans. The right was bestowed because in the past, when disaster struck and people were wiped out financially, they were carted off to debtor's prison.

There are two basic types of personal bankruptcy: one that totally wipes out your debts and the other that creates a payoff plan by which you pay your creditors a reduced amount (the amount is based upon what you can afford). You have your choice of either. If a payoff plan is chosen, the creditors have the plan shoved down their throat and do not have a true say in what you will be paying (within reason).

Does bankruptcy ruin your credit? Yes, but . . . believe it or not, some lenders don't mind dealing with people who have been in a bankruptcy—they believe the person has a sudden influx of available money because they are not paying their bills and better yet . . . it'll be another six years before the person can file bankruptcy again. The bottom line is that bankruptcy does ruin your credit, but there are a few creditors who might deal with you. And there are "secured" credit cards available where you give a credit-card company a sum of money, say $1000, and they give you a $1000 line of credit. The purpose of these cards is to give "plastic" to people who need it for renting a car, a truck when they move, or other situations where it's hard to deal with cash.

The issue is not what path you take to get back onto your feet in terms of your personal finances but to learn from the experience and not have to suffer the embarrassment and mental trauma again.

A few words from Robert Frost says a lot about most of us and money:

Never ask of money spent
Where the spender thinks it Went
Nobody was ever meant
To remember or invent
What he did with every cent.

Credit Security Checklist

1. Never give personal information to telephone solicitors. If you want to donate to a charity, tell them to bill you rather than giving them credit-card information over the telephone.
2. Get a copy of your credit report periodically and review it to verify the information. Think of it as a checkup on your credit health.
3. Avoid writing your credit-card number and social security number on your checks when making payment. On the one hand it may help the credit company if the check and payment coupon get separated. On the other hand, it puts critical information (your name, address, telephone number, bank address, bank account number, and credit or social security number) on one little piece of paper that passes through many hands.
4. Tear up preapproved credit applications that you are not going to accept so no one else accepts them!
5. Check your bills each month. We periodically come across other people's charges on our accounts. I once used another person's credit card for a month, and he used mine, because a waiter mixed up the cards in a restaurant.
6. Reduce the number of credit cards you carry. But keep one more for emergencies. . . .
7. Report credit-card losses immediately. With the advent of pay-at-pump and service-sta-

tion minimarts selling a wide variety of merchandise, someone with a lost or stolen gas card can rack up a sizable amount in no time. There are laws limiting your liability, both federally and in most states, but don't depend on the law because you never known when it will bite you.

8. Consider signing up with a company that notifies your credit-card provider in case of loss. If you have a large number of credit cards, it's a good idea.

9. Make a list of all your credit-card numbers and the "800" notification numbers you call in case of loss.

10. Stay conscious of the people around you when you use a credit card at a public phone.

11. Personal shredders have hit the market and are relatively cheap. Many people are buying them to shred the huge amount of paperwork that they toss in the can each month because there is a growing threat from thieves who retrieve information from the trash.

12. Photocopy both sides of your credit cards, bank cards, driver's license, insurance cards, passport, etc., and place the copies in a safe-deposit box.

6

Sexual Harassment

Typical Jury Instructions on Sexual Harassment:

The plaintiff seeks to recover damages based upon a claim of sexual harassment arising out of a business, service or professional relationship. The essential elements of a claim are:

1. There was a business, service or professional relationship between the plaintiff and defendant;
2. The defendant has made sexual advances, solicitations, sexual requests or demands for sexual compliance by the plaintiff;
3. Such conduct by the defendant was unwelcome by the plaintiff and was persistent or severe, continuing after a request by the plaintiff to stop;
4. Plaintiff was unable to easily terminate the relationship without tangible hardship; and
5. Such conduct by the defendant caused plaintiff to suffer injury, damage, loss, or harm.

Sexual harassment has a broad potential basis and can arise out of an incredible number of acts, ranging from outrageously making sex with the boss a requirement for job tenure to just crude or rude behavior. Legal definitions talk about "unwelcome sexual advances, requests for sexual favors, physical or verbal conduct of a sexual nature," but the definition is so broad that almost any conduct, from leering at a woman in a tight sweater to telling a joke with any kind of sexual connotations, may qualify.

This is a controversial and highly explosive area. While the laws apply equally to both sexes, complaints are generally from women and about men. Most of the complaints have a basis that is easy for anyone to understand—typical fact patterns are a male superior at work making sexual advances to a female employee; a group of good-old boys at the job pick on a female employee who has invaded their turf; a male employee makes offensive comments or touches a female employee.

The more controversial situations are when the current office joke with a sexual innuendo gets told freely around the office until it stops at the desk of a woman who cries foul. The man telling the joke angrily cries foul, too, saying he told the joke to forty other men and women and no one complained, yet this woman put in a complaint. Usually the complaint has been made for good reasons—being subjected to locker-room humor is neither in the job description or in good taste. But sometimes the complainer is just mean-spirited, overreacting, or out for revenge for some other reason.

I have been consulted a number of times on sexual-harassment matters, by women on the receiving end and men on the giving end. My experience has been that most of the complaints were justified. I've heard horror stories of women victimized at work, but there are people who will abuse anything, and on rare occasions I've seen some women on the job or with landlords use the accusation to accomplish some objective other than to redress true harassment (ranging from revenge to a reason not to be fired or not to pay the rent). These people have given a very necessary and vital legal principle a bad name.

It doesn't matter how innocent a joke or comment may sound to us, *if there is any sexual connotation, we shouldn't say it.* If an employee of the opposite sex walks into our office, and says, "Can I do something for you?" and we reply, "Sure, what are you doing tonight?" we have exposed ourselves to a sexual-harassment complaint.

Even male employees telling off-color jokes to other male employees and overheard by a female employee can be the subject of a sexual-harassment complaint and discipline.

A female employee telling dirty jokes, making advances, or making statements of a sexual nature to a male employee can be the subject of a complaint. (I have to say that no matter how "equal" we all are, men are more likely to be the culprits in these sexual-harassment situations—I mention later on that I've always wondered why 90 percent of the people in jail are men and this is another one of those situations—either men have dirtier mouths than women, or they just stick their foot in their mouth more.)

"Innocent" brushing against another employee, especially when the real motive isn't so innocent, can be the subject of a complaint.

Complaints have even arisen from situations in which the two employees involved have dated and one of them wants to terminate the relationship and the other creates emotional pressure at work.

There is only one way to deal with sexual-harassment issues on the job: Never, ever, under any circumstances, say, touch, tell a joke, or give a look, with any sexual connotation to anyone of the opposite sex. (Obviously, you could have a same-sex problem, too, depending on the circumstances.)

Just don't do it.

7

Buying or Selling a Home

*His name was George F. Babbitt. He was
forty-six years old now in April, 1920, and he
made nothing in particular, neither butter nor
shoes nor poetry, but he was nimble in the
calling of selling houses for more than people
could afford to pay.*

—Sinclair Lewis, *Babbitt*

Work with real-estate people, cooperate, but take
responsibility to check out comparables yourself.
When you're selling, get three opinions as to the
value of your residence. When you're buying, get
at least four different types of inspections done
and accompany the inspectors during their inspections so they can answer questions—just because they report on their form that the roof isn't
leaking doesn't mean that you might not have to
replace it in a short time.

Buying a home is usually the largest financial decision most
people will make in their lifetime. And I am appalled at how

so many times what should be the thrill of a lifetime ends up being a can of worms. For a quick refresher course on *how not* to buy a house, rent an old Cary Grant movie called *Mr. Blandings Builds His Dream House*. It is a wonderful movie about how a smart city slicker got taken by a bunch of country yokels (*The Money Pit* is a modern version).

Most people understand the three criteria that have to be considered in buying any home (house, co-op, condominium, vacation property, or a chicken farm): *location, location, location.* When you ignore those three magic words, you spread yourself out to be walked on. The Taj Mahal in a mediocre neighborhood wouldn't have a good resale value.

And they generally know what price they can qualify for (I said *qualify* for, not necessarily afford).

Where home deals commonly go wrong is in not doing our homework and getting a complete picture. The following are typical problems I've been consulted about over the years or have ran into myself:

If you are selling a home, don't sign a long-term agreement with a listing agent. Ninety days is usually enough because if you have a bad market and a good agent, you can always renew the listing. If the agent can't sell the home in that amount of time, knowing that the listing is expiring, you should probably move on. People will tell you that your agent doesn't matter because you will be on multiple listings, but it does matter because the agency you sign with is eager to sell your home themselves to "double-end" the commission (i.e., get both the buyer and selling agent's commission).

If you are selling your home, have agents from two or three different real-estate firms inspect the home and give you their opinion about the salability and pricing of the home. Get agents in the area. Someone from across town is not as likely to show your home as frequently as the agent a few blocks away. You rely upon a real-estate agent to price your home, just as you rely on a lawyer for legal advice and a doctor for medical . . . but all three professions are *arts*, not sciences, and the quality of the advice will often vary. If you had a serious legal or medical problem you would (or should) get a second opinion. There is no reason why you shouldn't get other opinions about your home.

Obviously, you should not necessarily go with the agent who has priced your home the highest—the agent may be way off on the price or using a high price to get you to sign up. Use some common sense and go with the agent who strikes you as the most likely to bring buyers in the door.

Regardless of whether you are selling or buying, have your agent give you a list of comparables and do a drive-by yourself to check them out. While you can generally trust real-estate people to take care of pricing and availability, you have a responsibility to be knowledgeable because not only are you the one who will ultimately make the decision, it's your money at risk.

Check out your neighbors. Look at the way they maintain their yards, the cars they drive, the upkeep on their homes. Come by on the weekends when people are likely to be home. Stop and talk to someone about the neighborhood. If you see Harley Hogs on the front lawns, guys with big hairy arms and tattoos, and girls with buck knives, maybe you should consider another neighborhood. . . .

Drive around the whole area, not just the particular neighborhood. A good neighborhood near a bad area is tainted— drug addicts and gangbangers have cars (in large metro areas there may be no such thing as a crime-free neighborhood).

If you have concerns about schools, check out the schools by going there and talking to people in administration. Just a walk down a hallway can tell you a lot about a school.

Check out transportation—freeway on- and off-ramps, bus and subway stations. If you're not familiar with the area, make sure you know how long it will take you to get to work.

Make several visits to the residence to make a walk-through. You will notice something different each time. Don't worry about making a nuisance of yourself—the seller wants to close a deal, and the agent wants a commission. Buying a residence is a major decision and give it the thought and consideration it is entitled to.

Don't *panic* when the salesperson calls and tells you there is another offer on the place. This is the oldest sales trick in the book. There probably is another offer. And it may sell to the other person. But do you want to pay more than someone else just because they want it, too? And do you want to jump into something that you may regret just because someone else wants the same place? You were looking for a home when you found this one—there'll be another one down the road that will fit the bill (and if there isn't, you'll hear about it from your spouse for the next forty years).

Have four types of inspections done: the standard termite/dry-rot inspection (which sometimes includes checking the roof and other areas for water damage), an appliance inspection (dishwasher, stove, heating, and air-conditioning, hot-water tank, purified-water system), a structural inspection (not just cracks and foundation—get an idea of the age and viability of the plumbing, electrical, roof, security system, garage-door opener), and your own inspection.

Be there when inspections are done—a simple check mark on a structural report that the roof is not leaking *now* does not tell you whether you will have to put out thousands of dollars for a new roof next year. Find out how old the roof is and when it will probably have to be replaced. Find out how old the plumbing is. When you go to the inspections, have a list of questions. Take notes. If you have any doubts, follow up with a letter to the inspector or your agent.

If you are buying a home in a new development, *find out what was on the land before.* In our crowded world, the past occupant could have been cows or chemical-waste disposal—you don't want to raise kids that glow in the dark.

Make sure that your lists of wants include everything you want the seller to leave behind. While it is not likely the seller will rip the air-conditioning ducts out of the walls, there are frequent hassles over items like drapes, blinds, shutters, bookcases, fireplace equipment, antennas and dishes, awnings, garage cabinets, fancy mailboxes, and even trees and shrubs. There may even be a piece of artwork or statue that works perfectly with the home or yard and you want it included.

When buying a co-op or a condo, go over the rules and conditions (CC&Rs) of the homeowners association. When you buy into one of these units, you are sharing space with others and bound by a set of bylaws. Make sure you can live with them. One of my clients bought a vacation home intending to rent it out to vacationers part of the year—only to find out that the covenants and conditions of the association forbade short-term renting. Another bought a condo as a retirement residence—only to be assessed thousands of dollars for a roof before she even moved in.

Ask questions and get the answers in *writing.* Before buying into a shared arrangement, you want to know what assessments have been levied over the past several years and what is planned for the future. High-ticket items like roofs should be dealt with. You also need to know whether there are widespread structural or water-damage problems anywhere in the complex that could result in you being assessed.

Make sure that all terms and conditions are in writing. Standard real-estate purchase contracts have blank places to be filled. Verbalize your concern to your agent, make sure they become part of the written offer, and that the entire sale is contingent upon your satisfaction with the response from the seller.

This business about "contingencies" is one of the most important points you need to know about buying a residence. In most locales, an offer to buy is usually contingent upon the buyer qualifying for a loan and getting satisfactory loan terms. Contracts generally lay out what interest rate and length of the mortgage the buyer will accept. That is because qualifying and being able to pay are such critical terms. But many terms may be of importance to you, yet failure of the seller to meet them may not be grounds to let the buyer out of the agreement. If you are concerned about the roof or the dishwasher, make sure that you have a right to back out of the agreement if you aren't able to come to terms with the seller about these items.

Keep one basic premise in mind about dealing with real estate: If it isn't written in the contract, it probably isn't going to be enforceable. I have represented home owners defrauded in a sale where terms were oral and obtained punitive damages against the agents and sellers—but that is rare.

Sit down with pencil and paper, with friends, family, and spouse, and make lists of everything you want to check out. And then make sure your want list (or the reasonable portions thereof) gets into the agreement. And include everything you expect the seller to leave behind if the items are not reflected in the agreement.

If you are being reasonable, most agents and sellers will work with you. And if they don't want to, walk away because it may be a can of worms.

In buying a residence, don't go into it as if it were World War III, but at the very least know your rights and make sure the agreement reflects your understanding of exactly what you are getting.

Buying/Selling Home Checklist

1. Don't sign a long-term listing agreement with an agent. Ninety days is usually enough. You can always renew.
2. If you are selling, get an opinion on the value of your home from two or three different agents.
3. Buyers and sellers should get a list of comparables and check them out personally.
4. Walk the property with the home inspectors. Have a list and ask questions about the foundation, roof, plumbing, electrical, heating and air, and all other significant items. Find out not just their condition, but their estimated age and life span.
5. Make sure *all* your "wants" are in the real-estate contract. Don't let any significant item get ignored. Terms left out of the agreement are probably not enforceable.
6. Review a seller's disclosure statement before making an offer.
7. Ask for a homeowner's protection policy to cover built-in appliances and air and heating units.

8

Buying a Car

Never fight fair with a stranger, boy. You'll never get out of the jungle that way.
—Arthur Miller, *Death of a Salesman*

There is one simple rule about buying a car: You are going to be taken if you don't know how to get the best price. Even if you are not the type to duke it out on a showroom floor with a fast-talking salesperson and the closer whose knuckles hit the floor, there are ways to get a decent deal.

The purchase of a car is one of the biggest financial moves many people make. And anyone who thinks it is easy probably gets taken. There is no industry where lies come easier and the bullshit flows faster than on a car lot. But even though it's not easy, and it's not pleasant if you are going to get a reasonable price, there are ways to reduce the hassle so you don't have the impulse to grab an assault rifle or end up grabbing your heart as you have a coronary on the showroom floor.

I have had a lifetime grudge against car salespeople dating from the time I was taken advantage of on my first purchase and I admit that I go out of my way to get the best deal. But that should be the objective for all of us regardless of whether you have a passion for getting the best deal or just hate getting taken. I have a friend who actually bought two new cars, one for herself and one for her daughter, at the same time, and paid the *sticker price* for both.

If you are not the type that wants to negotiate personally and don't have someone who can negotiate for you, you should consult one of the many firms that act as a middleman for the buyer and obtain what the industry calls "fleet prices." As professionals these people get reasonable prices on cars and pass the savings on to you along with their fee.

I always consult a couple of these firms to get their bottom line when I am negotiating for a car, and I have always beaten their price, but that's because I was willing to negotiate.

If you are going to negotiate, you need to start with a basic premise: You will never know how much or how little the dealership is making on the deal. The salesperson can tell you they are losing their shirt, the closer can whip out the actual factory invoice on the vehicle, and you will still be in the dark because dealers and manufacturers have a complex system of pricing and rebates between them, and the individual invoice on a car can be meaningless.

Collateral to that premise is that you cannot believe anything the salespeople tell you or the ads that are run. An ad will indicate that a car is being offered at an extremely low price—but reading it carefully you will find that in a city of eight million people there may be only *one* car at that price (and the sales manager already sold it to a brother-in-law) or that the car does not have an expensive feature (air-conditioning, automatic transmission) that you want. I'm not telling you that cars don't go on sale—sometimes they do, but most of the "sales" are nothing more than bait-and-switch tactics to get you into the dealership.

Knowing that you are operating in the dark as to what the dealer's profit will be, your only safe bet is to go with the "low bid" from a number of dealers. How do you get bids going? It's very easy.

You start by selecting the car of your choice, not just the model and color, but *everything*, from the type of radio and seat covering down to the type of hubcaps. You have to include every possible optional feature or you will not be getting a bid from Dealer A on the same car as the one from Dealer B.

You need to write these items down and list the nonnegotiable items (like the model and color) and the items that are not as important to you.

You obtain this information by going to dealers and checking cars and test driving until you hit exactly what you want. It's okay to talk to salespeople—just don't buy into their act. When they tell you that they can get you a special deal on this one car this one time at this exact moment because their manager needs *this* sale to make a quota and is willing to literally give the car away . . . and your heart starts pumping and your throat gets dry and you know you're going to burst if you don't buy that car . . . take a deep breath, smile, nod, tell them you left something in the oven at home and that you'll be back later and then run as fast as you can off the lot. (It's not polite to tell salespeople that they are full of crap—they are doing the best job they can in a tough industry. While you shouldn't beat up on them for trying, don't let them take you by talking you into a bad deal.)

Once you have defined exactly what you want to buy, call the various salespeople you've met during your car search and ones at other dealers and tell them exactly what you want and ask them to give you their best price. Let them know that you are ready right now to buy the car and will be over immediately to close the deal.

Many people believe that by telling the salesperson they will pay cash for the car they get a better deal. This was true in the past, but today most dealers "participate" in the profit from financing (i.e., the more interest you pay, the more money they get) and would rather see you finance a car than pay for it outright.

I try to get five "bids." If you are trying to buy a much-sought-after car, you will find the bids are all very similar and you are wasting your time trying to get a lower price.

Once you have established the rock-bottom price—get it confirmed in writing. I mentioned an incident in which a salesman accused me of costing him his job and I told him I'd get his license, too (instead of costing him his job, he probably got a bonus from the dealer for aggravating another customer). The incident was precipitated by the fact that the salesman *and* his manager had both verbally agreed over the phone to a price and then refused me the price when I arrived at the dealership. Since that incident, I fax the salesperson my exact specs and the price and have him sign the fax and return it to me before I go to the dealership. I make sure that the exact terms, down to the penny, out the door, *everything included,* are on the fax.

Think that completely solves the problem? No, because they have more tricks up their sleeves. When they hand us those dozen pages of small print to sign and initial, it is impossible for any of us to read or even understand most of it. But our eye will pick up items that are handwritten into the blanks and we tend to make sure those items conform to the deal we made. Dealers long ago caught on to this and many now have hidden costs (such as a dealer-prep charge or an end of lease fee) *printed* on the form. Because it is printed, our eye slips by it.

This is where your list stating the exact terms and the bottom-line price comes in. Don't argue. Don't get mad. Just tell them these are the terms, and you will not pay a cent more. If that kills the deal, walk out.

Yelling, getting upset, shouting at the idiots does absolutely no good (although I find it sometimes does wonders for my blood pressure). Just stay calm and point out the fact that you are not paying a cent more than agreed and be willing to leave when they try to put the screws to you.

There are a couple of other points to keep in mind.

As I mentioned above, if you are trying to buy a hot car, negotiating does very little good. It's not uncommon for salespeople to have waiting lists for some cars. By a "hot" car I am referring to something in high demand and low supply—they are not necessarily the best-selling cars and are often cars that are popular with only a small segment of the market. Usually the most popular cars are in the greatest supply because that's what the factory is cranking out.

Timing is also critical—to us and the dealer. Most of us are not going to wait for January for a better deal just because cars sell for less than they do in August—when we need or want the car, that's the time we are going for it. But you can use short-term timing to your benefit. It's okay to go around and look at cars on weekends and holidays, but don't buy one then. My choices are in the mornings on Tuesday, Wednesday, and Thursday. My experience has been that the salespeople have full bellies on Saturdays and Sundays, are still closing deals on Monday, are feeling a little hungry on Tuesday, are desperate on Wednesday, are still hungry but can look forward to the weekend on Thursday, and are starting to hop by Friday.

Early in the morning on a dark and rainy Wednesday in

February is a great time to buy a car (except for those of us who *want it now!*).

You also get a better response on your requests for bids midweek, when the salespeople are less busy.

A willingness to buy "leftovers" also gets you a better price. A particular color, a feature (such as two-wheel drive in a sports vehicle), or just the fact that the car didn't sell well and the dealers are stuck with them, can get you a rock-bottom deal. (I have a personality defect that keeps me from taking advantage of these deals—I want what I want and I won't take a different color or feature.)

Avoid buying cars without a track record for its engine. Consumer-type reports are good for tracking the maintenance history of cars after the car has been out a couple of years, but prior to that the data may not be available. The car you are attracted to may be the sharpest-looking beast on the road, but if it breaks down frequently or has performance problems, you are going to sour on it and find that its trade-in value is lower than what you hoped for.

Doing research on the car you want to buy is also a good idea. Don't forget that the local library will not only have a dozen magazines on cars, but will have books on the subject. You can learn a great deal about the car you are interested in and competitive models from these sources.

If you are interested in a used car, keep in mind that the best value is usually a two-year-old model. Try to find one being returned on a two-year lease because people who lease cars have to take good care of them and stay within mileage limits or pay extra. Most leases are three years, and these cars should also be a consideration.

If you are offered a car that has been kept by its previous owner for less than two years, ask yourself why. While some people buy a new car each year, and others get their car repossessed for failure to pay, the car might have ended back in the dealership's hands because it is a lemon. Find out why the car was returned and ask the dealer for the name and phone number of the previous owner so you can contact them.

If you are privately selling a car, never take a personal check—your best bet is to have the buyer meet you at the department of motor vehicles (or an auto club outlet if you are a member) with a cashier's check. That way you are not only guaranteed your money, but you can get title transferred immediately. In many states just signing over the "pink slip" and giving up the keys legally passes title, but that does not mean you are not going to get sued if your name is still officially on title at the motor-vehicle department because the buyer did not get around to changing title—or is avoiding paying out the transfer fees and taxes. While you may ultimately get yourself out of a lawsuit, proving your position may be expensive.

Checklist on Buying a Car

1. If you don't want to negotiate, go to a firm that specializes in making deals for consumers. And before buying with them, compare their price with the dealer's.
2. If you are willing to negotiate, get a price from several dealers. Don't expect miracles if you are trying to buy a car in great demand and short supply.
3. If you get a price from several dealers, make sure they are giving you a price on the car you want to buy—have every single detail about the car written down—model, color, and other features right down to the hubcaps.

4. If you have access to a fax machine, confirm the deal in writing before you go out to the dealership.
5. Avoid trying to make a deal on weekends and holidays when the car lots are swamped.
6. Check out the car you want in consumer magazines and books.
7. On a high-quality used car, don't buy it if maintenance records aren't included.
8. When you get elated because you have just put the screws to the dealer, pinch yourself, because you're dreaming. . . .

Lemons

I've handled many "lemon" situations for clients and have arbitrated and sued for clients stuck with a bad car. Cars are a very emotional issue for many people. Our home may be important, but it's the car that keeps us moving to earn the rent or house payment. And many people are "car" people who really have their hearts into their car, and when the car is ailing, it's like having a sick child.

Getting a lemon is no fun, nor is it easy to deal with because the deck is stacked against you.

Basically, there are three paths available in regard to lemons: going through the manufacturer's plan, invoking your rights under a lemon law, and suing.

Most car manufacturers have instituted procedures that specify how the owner of a new car can handle the problem. These procedures typically require that you keep taking the car back and having it repaired. Sometimes there is an arbitration or mediation procedure to follow. In addition, most states have "lemon laws" that establish a procedure by which you can invoke your rights under the statutes. This, too, generally involves an arbitration or mediation procedure.

Regardless of whether you use the manufacturer's procedure or your state's law, the information you need to gather in order to win involves the same facts. Please note this: *Most of these cases are won by the manufacturers and that happens because people simply do not know how to go about enforcing their rights.*

The typical and very human response from new-car buyers who find that their dream car is sick is to respond emotionally with frustration, anger, and hurt. I have news for you—if you thought the salespeople were the biggest bandits at the dealership, you're in for a surprise when you start dealing with the service people. (Did you know that your friendly, concerned service advisor is probably on *commission* instead of drawing an hourly wage?)

Understand this basic concept in dealing with large entities such as car manufacturers (lemons are usually a manufacturer's problem even if the local dealer is handling it) and government entities: They have inflexible criteria. What that means is that certain "rules" have been set up at the upper echelon and legal department and the people you are dealing with—at the dealership or on the phone to the manufacturer or in a government office—have no authority to change the rules.

If your problem fits the criteria for the relief you want, you will get the relief—and if it doesn't, they are locked into denying it.

The trick is to get your problem to fit the criteria.

You can scream, you can blow up, you can threaten them with lawyers and spend several hundred dollars having your lawyer send them a letter. You can even take them to arbitration, but unless you understand that you are dealing with "rules" etched in stone, and your problem has to fit into the criteria, you will lose.

Most people fail to comprehend this basic premise. They are angry, feel ripped off, and believe they are entitled to get the new, perfect-running car that was contemplated in the purchase. In other words, they expect justice. Unfortunately, justice is not the name of the game. Rather, it is a numbers game.

The manufacturers' arbitration boards and lemon laws all have a numerical solution: You have to have a certain number and certain type of problem over a designated period of time during which the dealer has had the opportunity but failed to remedy the defect. In other words, you have to give the dealer a reasonable number of attempts at fixing it. This would be a typical scenario for many locales: If in the first 12,000 miles of ownership, you have made a "reasonable" number of attempts to have the dealer repair a warrantied problem and the car cannot be repaired, you are entitled to a replacement vehicle. What is considered to be reasonable varies—some states say that there is a presumption if you had the car in for the same defect a specified number of times (usually three or four times) during a specified period (usually the first 12,000 miles) or the car has been out of service for a specific number of days (fifteen days in some states, thirty days in others). Generally, the problem has to relate to the use, value, or safety of the vehicle and not to minor defects.

While this may sound easy, where almost everyone fails is in *documenting* the problem. They cannot prove that the car has been in for the specific problem because the service orders don't reflect it, or they have failed in returning the car and racking up the number of required days that it has to be down.

Letting the car sit in your driveway while you make

angry calls to the dealer or the manufacturer's 800 number gets you exactly no points when you are facing an arbitrator and are asked to prove your case. How do you prove it? *With service orders that meet the criteria set by the law or the manufacturer.*

Because of the high cost of lawyers and litigation, and the fact that car problems usually involve "thousands" of dollars rather than "tens of thousands," it may not be financially sound to expect a lawyer to handle your problem all the way through. But at the very least, at an early stage before your time runs out on giving the dealer an opportunity to repair, consult an attorney to understand the "rules" you must comply with.

Checklist on Handling a Lemon

1. Keep your cool and build your case. Be polite but firm in verbalizing your complaints to the service people and check the service order to make sure all of your complaints are listed. Don't blame the order taker for a defect that originated in Detroit, Frankfurt, or Tokyo.
2. Find out exactly what the criteria are that you have to meet in order to get the car replaced.
3. Meet the criteria by taking the car back for repairs for the number of times required or for the number of days required.
4. Document, document, and document the case even more. While a diary of events (including dates, times, phone numbers, and names) helps, the real proof of the pudding is the service orders.

5. If you didn't get advice at the onset of your problem, spend a couple of hundred dollars to lay it out for a lawyer and get some feedback. In some metro areas, there are law firms that actually specialize in lemon law. Unless you find one of these specialty law firms, it may be difficult to have a lawyer handle the matter all the way through for you because the cost will be too high.

6. Don't rack up months and mileage without documenting the problem by visits to the dealer. In most states the lemon nature of the vehicle must be proven in the first twelve months and/or 12,000 miles, but you need to check the exact requirements for your locale.

9

Nuisance Calls

Hello, Neil and Buzz. I'm talking to you by telephone from the Oval Room at the White House, and this certainly has to be the most historic telephone call ever made.

—Richard Nixon, speaking to the
first men on the moon

The telephone has opened our homes for an army of salespeople, hustlers, and charities. Remember that it's your phone, and you don't have to listen. Even if you want to buy or contribute to a charity, tell the caller to send the information to you by mail to make sure it is legitimate. And don't give your address. If they don't already have your address, they don't need it. . . .

I don't think there is anyone who hasn't picked up the telephone and heard the person on the other end of the line say, "Sorry, I have the wrong number." Usually it is just a misdialed number, but once in a while these people will say, "Who's this?" My reply invariably is, "Who's *this*?"

I am not trying to be a wise guy; I make that reply for two reasons: Strangers who call my home and ask "who's this" are being impolite, and I don't want to give out information as to who I am to strangers.

The telephone in general has become an invasion of privacy and a source of annoyance. I try to be polite when a telephone salesperson calls. I usually half listen until there is a pause for breath and then tell them I am sorry and not interested. And I am usually polite to wrong-number callers, asking them to tell me the number they are calling so they don't redial me by accident.

One caller I am not polite to is a dirty caller. I have received a half dozen of these calls for some sort of karmic reason. And I never let them finish their remarks. To be honest I interrupt the call with a disgusting remark about their manhood and hang up. None of them ever call back. My suggestion, however, is for you not to contribute to the bad language on the telephone network and simply hang up without saying a word. Don't get shocked, don't reply back, don't let your disgust or anger show, just hang up. These people feed on shock and love it when they can engage you in a dialog.

If you have the calling-party ID feature on your telephone, make a note of the number and report it to the police.

If you get repetitive nuisance calls, report it to the telephone company and the police. In this day of computerized telephone service, it is quite easy for the telephone company to put a tracer on nasty calls.

A type of nasty call I have been on both sides of are harassing calls from ex-lovers and spouses. I have represented the callers and the callees (sometimes these calls are repetitive middle-of-the-night hang-ups). When they get too bad, the police put a tracer on the calls and track them back to the caller and file charges. This is a form of electronic stalking—don't do it.

You should make sure that everyone in the household, including children, knows how to react to strangers on the telephone. They should never give out their name, never identify who is in the house, in fact, never engage in a telephone conversation other than to listen politely to a sales pitch before saying good-bye and hanging up.

The way to handle intruders on the telephone, whether they are honest salespersons or criminals, is to remember a basic premise: It is your house, your telephone, and you have control.

You should never accept unsolicited offers for merchandise or charitable contributions over the telephone. No matter what the person on the other end of the line says, the fact is that you do not know for sure with whom you are dealing.

If you want to buy the merchandise or want to make a contribution, ask them to send the offer in the mail. Don't give them your address. Most firms already have it. If they don't, just don't give it to them anyway. If you are desperate to contribute, give them a business address. Or take a deep breath and tell them good-bye and hang up. In a pinch, you could ask for an 800 number to call back to verify that it is a legitimate vendor or charity.

10

Auto Accidents

ACCIDENT: *an unpleasant and unintended happening, sometimes resulting from negligence, that results in injury, loss, damage, etc.*
—Webster's Dictionary

What to do at the scene to protect your rights, how to deal with the other party, witnesses, the police, your insurance company, their insurance company, and with the repair shop. Checklist covers gathering information at the accident scene to getting the car repaired and the claim paid. Where people who are not at fault in accidents fail most at the scene of an accident is getting witnesses. By the time they get out of their car and look at the damages and speak to the other driver, the witnesses are miles away. I also recommend carrying a cheap, disposable camera in the car and taking pictures before the cars are moved . . . if you are not at fault.

In our car-dominated society, we drive miles to a gym to spend a few minutes on an exercise bike or a treadmill. A "bad car day" ranks just beneath nuclear holocaust when it keeps us from getting to work or to an appointment. Those who own cars live in fear of our insurance companies—we will lie, cheat, pay off claims out of our own pocket, sell our bodies on the street, do anything to keep from having to put in a claim and cause the insurance company we have been paying for years to put out a few dollars (we know our insurance company will punish us later if we've been bad).

I have had successful executives in my office trying frantically to figure out some way to get around putting in an insurance claim.

Coming fender-to-fender with people also gives one some insight as to how greedy and abusive some people are. And there are some wonderful people you bump into by accident. (I'd like to relate a story to you about how I got into *two* accidents, neither my fault, in five minutes in Naples, Italy, and how two gorillas who could not speak a word of English—which matched my ability at Italian—took care of the whole matter for me and kissed my hand at that, but my wife, who was there and knows it's true, insists no one would believe it, so I won't tell you about it.)

In this section we will deal with specifics on what you need to know and do at the scene of an accident, but first you should be aware of some important factors that we don't usually think about.

Accidents commonly result in what lawyers and judges call "a liar's contest" because both parties are claiming they were in the right. For example, the light was green for only one of them, but both claim they had the green. Surprisingly, I find many times that both are telling the truth—*as they see it*. I have personally been involved in one accident in which I was the cause. Deep in thought about something, I went through a red light and got hit broadside by another driver. If I had not had a passenger in the car who yelled at the last moment that I was going through a red light, no one would have been able to convince me that I was the one at fault. Even the "facts" looked to be in my favor—the other driver broadsided my car. Over the years, in questioning people about what happened in accidents, I have come to the conclusion that many people honestly believe they were not at fault and in fact really don't know how the accident happened because if they were aware they were making a negligent movement with their car, they would have avoided the accident.

But don't get the idea that everyone out there is denying responsibility in good faith. For every decent person who takes responsibility for their acts, there are several who deny! deny! deny! when they are at fault.

The second generality has to do with taking responsibility at the scene for the accident. Insurance companies and lawyers will tell you to keep your mouth shut at the scene. If there is any doubt at all about liability or if the accident is so serious criminal charges may arise, that is good advice. But for the typical fender-bender, not taking responsibility aggravates the matter. Knowing that I had caused the accident by blowing the red light, when the other driver got out of his mangled car yelling, I calmed him down by assuring him that I was at fault, called for a tow truck for both of us, and took him down the street to rent a car. When I called in the claim, the insurance adjuster intimated that I had been too "nice" and I told him it had nothing to do with being nice—I had caused the problem and it was my responsibility to take care of it.

The other driver, by the way, was a decent person. Injured enough to seek medical advice, he never put a claim in for bodily injury and that saved me a great deal of money (the insurance company gives one "free" fender-bender but raises the rates if an injury is claimed). More important than the money, he became a friend.

I think you know how the scenario would have gone if I had played games about who was at fault.

When you are not at fault in an accident, the most important thing in your life (assuming there are no serious injuries) is *proving* it. To prove it, and avoid the liar's-contest scenario, you need witnesses. Pinning down witnesses is your most urgent task. Don't delay because in a few seconds the people in cars around you will be a mile away. I have had three fender-benders in which I was not at fault and in each of them I immediately had the people who caused the accident claiming I was at fault. I ignored them and went directly to the cars behind and people on the street to get names and phone numbers, turning the tables on the adverse drivers.

Because I live in a city with a "car culture" and spend so much of my life in a car, I carry a cheap, disposable camera in the glove compartment. I have needed it exactly once, but it saved me from a lawsuit: A woman "lane cheating" came down a metered parking lane and hit my car as I was turning. Traffic moved away quickly and I had no witnesses. But I took shots of my car and the car that hit me to show their position after the collision as evidence that she was in the wrong (naturally, she claimed the accident was my fault).

Specifics you need to keep in mind if you are involved in an accident are:

Try to remain calm. If the other driver is agitated, do not buy into the anger. Do not become confrontational under any circumstances. If the other driver is confrontational and a telephone is available, call the police. While the police generally do not respond to accidents in which there are no injuries (or minor injuries), advise the 911 operator that a police officer is necessary to maintain the peace.

Be careful getting out of your vehicle because other traffic may pose a hazard. If your vehicle is blocking traffic or is a hazard where it is, and it can be moved safely to the side of the road, move your vehicle. If not, leave the vehicle as it is since sometimes the position of the vehicles in the roadway can determine whether or not there was a right-of-way violation by one of the drivers.

After care of any immediate medical problems and getting the vehicles out of the way if they are a hazard, you need to obtain the following information involving the other party: name, address, and telephone number of driver (and owner, if different); driver's license number, license plate number, and make of car; name of insurance company and policy number of driver (and owner, if different); name, address, and telephone number of any witnesses. (See checklist at the end of the chapter.)

As mentioned earlier, it's critical to get the information about witnesses. Some people are reluctant to give their names as witnesses because they don't want to get involved, so try to convince them it's the right thing to do. Even if they didn't see the actual impact, they may be able to help with the color of the traffic light, the point of impact, the position of the vehicles or any other information that might identify who was at fault.

If you're in an accident that involves damage to somebody else's vehicle or other property (such as a parked car), you have a duty to locate and notify the owner or person in charge of the damaged property. You should provide your name and address and a brief description of what happened. This is commonly done by placing a note in the windshield. To avoid being labeled a "hit-and-run" driver when your piece of paper blows away, notify the police department also (in many locales there is a duty to report the matter to the police anyway).

In regard to providing first aid to injured parties on the scene, don't give assistance unless you know what you are doing or unless it is a dire emergency. Pulling an injured person from a wrecked car and laying them on the ground so they can be comfortable may seem like a good idea, but if they have spinal injuries, the person could become paralyzed from your actions.

In most locales, you have a duty to report accidents involving bodily injury or significant auto damage to the motor-vehicle department or the police. Don't report the accident unless you have a duty to because the information can end up on your driving record and be obtained by an insurance company when you renew or change policies.

Failure to provide identifying information at the scene of an accident and leaving the scene is considered a hit-and-run, a criminal offense. The fact that there are criminals creating minor traffic accidents to get you to stop may motivate you to keep on going, but make sure you signal the other party to follow you to a safe, well-lit location (this situation is discussed at length in the chapter about crazies on the road).

Don't make any cash settlements on the spot—there may be damage under the carriage of the car or frame damage that you do not see.

In regard to insurance claims, see the chapter on that subject. The most common problem people run into on dealing with a claim is when their car is "totaled" and a dispute arises in determining the price. Adjusters use computerized programs to calculate damages but the "comparable" vehicles often are quite different in terms of mileage, condition, and accessories. You are generally entitled to the "retail" value of your vehicle, and your best approach is to obtain an appraisal from a dealership (who will be anxious to sell you a car to replace the damaged one) and to obtain ads from newspapers and other periodicals.

Remember that the adjuster has a file that has to be documented and a form to fill out. They cannot take your word for value or your emotional feelings about what the value should be—you have to give them documentation of the selling price of comparable vehicles.

Information Checklist

1. The names and telephone numbers of any witnesses (to be practical, if you are sure you are at fault, gathering witness information may not be in your best interest).
2. The name, address, and telephone number of the other driver.
3. The driver's license number of the other driver.
4. The name, address, and telephone number of the vehicle's owner if the driver is not the owner.
5. The make, model, and year of the other car.
6. The vehicle license number of the other driver's car.
7. Name of the insurance company and policy number of the other driver.
8. If a camera is available, and *if* you weren't at fault, take pictures of the cars before they are moved.
9. After you have finished talking to the other driver, write down any statements which constitute admissions of fault that the other driver made.

10. Write down specifics about the location—time, date, weather conditions, pertinent road and traffic conditions, the numerical address, and street names.
11. Notify your insurance company promptly.
12. If you have a duty to notify the police or department of motor vehicles, do so.

11

Insurance Claims

An insurance company is not your friend.

—The Author

There is a technique in dealing with insurance companies. You have to know how to provide what the company representatives need to document their files. When negotiations break down with the adjuster, you should go up the line of management within the company before resorting to a government agency. You need the right information before pressure can be applied. Insurance companies win the majority of complaints against them because people do not know what ammunition they need to succeed.

As I mentioned in the chapter on auto accidents, there are few things we pay so much for and fear to get any benefit from than insurance claims.

This is another area where there is intense resentment

from consumers and a feeling of helplessness, all for good reasons.

And most people use the wrong approach to insurance claims. They either roll over and play dead, expecting the company to treat them fairly, or they do a little fudging on their claim, justifying it on the grounds that the insurance company is going to cheat them anyway. Claims are usually an "audited accounting" more than anything else. You are claiming a certain dollar figure as damages and the company wants proof of the figures.

I have no comment to make about people cheating—and insurance companies giving the shaft to their insureds—except that I generally find in life that what goes around comes around.

In terms of trusting your insurance company, you can trust them less than you do your lawyer, doctor, or plumber. No matter what you see in the ads, none of them are out to do us any favors. You will generally find that small claims are treated fairly and expediently by most companies. But when you have a substantial claim, get ready to fight tooth and nail. They are among the toughest litigators in the world.

Every case in which I've sued an insurance company I've won for my client . . . but I've always lost a few fingers and toes in the fight.

Most people are under the misconception that their insurance company is on their side and that they will also be treated fairly by the company who insures the person who damages them. People who have never had an insurance claim or only had small claims usually have this fantasy. People who have had significant-sized claims are more apt either to be cautious about insurance companies or to outright hate them.

There is something about working for large companies that quite often dehumanizes people, especially when they are at the higher levels of management. Men and women who are pillars of their community and church or temple and who wouldn't steal a blade of grass from their neighbors get involved in price fixing, bribery of government officials, and gouging consumers. And people at much lower levels join the unethical and illegal conduct despite the fact that there isn't an extra dollar in their paycheck for it. They develop a "them against us" attitude, typical of people in the military and police forces, that dehumanizes the "thems."

We don't expect a bank or big car manufacturer to be on our side—we know they are large, impersonal corporations. But we *pay* an insurance company to back us up in an emergency, and too often the company protects its own financial interest at the expense of ours. And sometimes they are damn tricky. Early in my career I had a case in which a woman was standing by an above-the-ground backyard swimming pool when the pool suddenly "bulged," inundating her with water and crushing her ankle. She had an accident insurance policy, but the company refused to pay off. I contacted the department of insurance and received back a call from an insurance investigator who told me they had a number of complaints against the company because the policy benefits were so narrowly drawn—you could collect if you were injured in a burning building (it had to be *in* the burning building—the company had denied the claim of a man's family when the man had fallen from a burning building and died on the pavement), or *while* drowning.

After giving it some thought and looking up the definition of "drowning" in a dictionary and found it included being "inundated" by water, I made a claim against the policy for the injury to the ankle that occurred while my client was "drowning" under water pouring over her from the edge of the pool. I managed to collect for my client because the adjuster decided I was a determined fanatic who would take them all the way to the Supreme Court for the two-bit policy (and he was right).

But the main reason I collected was because I had found a way for the adjuster to pay the claim under a precise provision of the policy. He had a form that had to be filled out for every claim he paid. Those forms were reviewed by his boss and by periodic auditors reporting to upper management. The adjuster really had no authority—either I worded the demand correctly, or to keep his own job, he had to deny it.

Getting down to a more basic level, dealing with an insurance company is no different than dealing with any other large entity where the person you are actually having contact with, in this case telephone contact with an adjuster, has little or no *discretion* in terms of his or her authority.

We tell the adjuster our tale of woe. We expect sympathy, compassion, and a check in the mail, but what we get are demands for more and more information.

What most people don't understand is that the adjuster has a form he or she is dealing with. That form calls for the input of data from the insured. When the data matches the criteria for getting benefits, you'll get a check—usually. Some companies are notorious for refusing to pay even black-and-white claims, but in that case you should see an attorney.

What an insurance claim often comes down to is a subtle game in which you are trying to give the adjuster exactly what the adjuster needs.

In order to do that, you need to know exactly what benefits you are entitled to under the policy. None of us can interpret an insurance policy, so the best way to find out your benefits is to request that the adjuster send you a letter advising of the benefits you have available.

You should also request written instructions on exactly what information the company needs from you in order for you to comply (itemizations of damaged property, estimates of repair, proof of value, receipts for expenditures, etc.).

With an explanation of your benefits in hand, and an itemization of your losses that conforms to the adjuster's needs in terms of documenting the claim file, you will be able to resolve most claims without going through a major hassle.

When the hassle begins, you have to ask yourself if you have a strong position or whether it is just wishful thinking. A friend came to me when his car was totaled in an accident and the adjuster only offered $8000 for the damages. The friend had paid much more than that just for refurbishing the car, and it was considered by collectors as a minor classic worth $25,000. But the computer program the insurance company used did not have a "classic" category—it had a "poor" condition, "good" condition, and "dealer" quality, but no category for a vehicle that was in short supply and high demand.

I tried to resolve the problem with the adjuster, but the adjuster was stuck with the criteria the company provided, and the classic car did not fit in the scheme of things. I went to the adjuster's supervisor and basically hit another blank wall. At this point I had to decide whether to appeal to the department of insurance. I did not because it is another bureaucratic organization and, frankly, I had another motive: If I made an insurance-department complaint, I risked having the insurance claims people going out of their way to win in order not to have the department of insurance find against them. Rather than starting a war over a relatively small matter, I told the supervisor that my client was going to call the department of insurance (which was true) and that I was trying to head the client off because I thought it was all too much hassle. The subtle threat, along with "comparables" showing the car's value, turned the supervisor around and got the claim settled at full value.

But bear this in mind: If I hadn't had the documentation the company required, or had approached the insurance-company personnel as a bully, I would not have gotten the claim settled without litigation. (There are plenty of attorneys who force problems into litigation to feather their own nest.)

A couple of more tips:

Watch your tone of voice. Certain occupations (police officers, insurance adjusters, telephone-company reps, etc.) get a lot of flack from the public, some of which is just outrageous and irrational. When you come across as excited or angry, they clam up or get uptight. When you get on the phone or face-to-face with these people, remember that they did not cause the problem and may have little control over resolving it. If you have been kicked to the point where you can't keep the tension out of your voice, disarm the other person a bit by telling them that you understand they did not cause the problem and your anger is not directed at them. When you deal with people in a bureaucracy, you want the people on your side because they are your only hope of getting what you want from the organization.

Another tool you have for dealing with an insurance company is to obtain a copy of your claims file. Most states require that a company provide you a copy of the claim file upon written demand. What the file will tell you is exactly what the company has done to investigate your claim and evaluate your damages. Often you will find that the adjuster has done very little.

If you are tired of hassling, sometimes a well-drafted letter to the regional vice president or the president of the insurance company helps. These people never see your letter but have underlings who send the letter down the line to the claims people. I usually target a regional vice president over the president because they do not get as many complaints as the president and tend to act upon them more expediently.

This is another area where you need to seek legal advice at an early stage.

If everything else fails, report the transgression to your insurance-company regulatory agency in a well-drafted letter backed up by all that documentation you have gathered.

Checklist for Dealing with an Insurance Claim

1. Don't approach the claim as mortal combat. Cooperate and provide all of the information requested. But keep in the back of your mind that while your claim will probably be treated fairly, an insurance company is not necessarily on your side, and you have to be cautious dealing with them.

2. The insurance adjuster needs certain information as proof of your claim and to document the company file. You are just spinning your wheels until you come up with the documentation.

3. Insurance companies are used to dealing with people who inflate their claim. Don't do it. It's dishonest and usually counterproductive.

4. Have the adjuster advise you in writing exactly what benefits are available for your claim.

5. Have the adjuster advise you in writing exactly what you need to provide in terms of proof to obtain the benefits.

6. Maintain a calm voice even if you want to rip the adjuster's throat out. It does no good to scream at these people. They just work there . . .

7. If you run into difficulties dealing with the adjuster, request, in writing, a copy of your claim file.

8. If you cannot resolve the claim with the adjuster, get the name and phone number of the supervisor. And then that person's supervisor. If you are not totally unreasonable, you will usually get the matter resolved with a supervisor. If you cannot do it on a lower level, appeal to a vice president or the president of the company.

9. File a complaint with the state insurance department only as a last resort. These agencies usually move slowly in resolving claims.

10. Don't be unreasonable. While it's true that insurance companies are notorious for trying to avoid paying claims or not paying all that they should on a claim, most companies deal fairly with most claims most of the time. On an ordinary claim, if you can't resolve it at the adjuster or claims-manager level, there is usually something wrong in terms of the information you are providing.

12

Dealing with Lawyers

A lawyer with a briefcase can steal more than a hundred men with guns.

—Mario Puzo, *The Godfather*

What to look for in a lawyer: When you are charged with a crime, look for an aggressive lawyer whom the prosecution has respect for (a pit bull with a brain). If you're in an accident, get a lawyer who has enough heart to make a jury cry and enough guts to take the case that far. In terms of business litigation, the best lawyers know how to resolve cases without worrying about what it's going to cost them in fees—and when the other side won't settle, they go for the jugular. In a divorce, watch out for the sharks to whom your misery is just more money to them and the social worker who may be ineffective in court—and when your spouse tries to take you to the mat, make sure you have a lawyer who isn't going to roll over and play dead.

There are about the same percentage of bad lawyers in this world as there are bad doctors, bad auto mechanics, and bad shoe salespersons. The difference between the occupations is the effect on your life: A bad lawyer can cost your money or your freedom. A bad pair of shoes gives you sore feet. A bad doctor can take your life.

To protect your money and your freedom, and in situations like divorce, where much happiness can ride on your lawyer's performance in a custody battle, you should know some of the rules lawyers play under. I will go through the various "types" of lawyers and give you tips on what to look for to win and how to avoid getting ripped off.

First, while other professions divide themselves up in specialties, like doctors and engineers, their methods and payment arrangements are basically the same. That's not true with lawyers.

The first difference between lawyers is that big-city lawyers tend to specialize in one area of the law and most small-town lawyers are "general" practitioners and have to know about a number of different subjects. I have been a small-town lawyer and a big-city lawyer, and on many occasions I found that my background and experiences handling a wide range of cases often meant more in a fight than an attorney who had superior knowledge on one issue but who never really grasped the whole picture. Small-town general-practice lawyers are frequently in court and know their way around the courtroom. In large cities there are great numbers of lawyers who have never done a trial.

One category of lawyers are called "plaintiffs' lawyers." These are attorneys who handle auto accidents, injuries due to defective products, and battles against insurance companies and large corporations. These lawyers are usually among the best in the country, but they get a bad press for two reasons: It's an area of law that attracts some of the worst lawyers, and the insurance companies have waged a publicity war to try to discredit them.

These attorneys typically take cases based upon "contingency fees," in which you do not pay up front but the lawyer takes a percentage, usually a third, of the recovery. The reason for the contingency fee system is that someone who has been injured can rarely hire a lawyer to sue the guilty party. When you read in the paper that an injured person received a multimillion-dollar award in a lawsuit against a car manufacturer for a defective gas tank that erupted in an accident and killed or horribly scarred the occupants, you can bet that a team of lawyers has hundreds of thousands of dollars in out-of-pocket trial expenses and thousands of hours of work on the case.

The thing to watch out for with this type of lawyer are the shysters. When I became an attorney over twenty years ago attorneys were forbidden to advertise because it demeaned the profession. The way you found a lawyer was to ask friends and relatives for a referral, the same way you find a doctor. To give consumers more choices and create more competition, the laws changed, and advertising is permitted in most states. However, it didn't accomplish either goal. What advertising did was throw open the door to people who have good business sense but may be awful lawyers. Friends and relatives are going to refer you to someone they got a good result from. When you get your "referral" from a yellow page ad or TV commercial, you are generally getting lawyers who deal with huge numbers of cases and turn the actual handling of files over to their staff. There have been revelations that some of these TV advocates have handled thousands of cases—without ever entering a courtroom. That means they are just taking whatever the insurance company offers, ripping off a big fee, and sending you the change that is left. Worse, the insurance companies offer these "legal mills" low dollar on claims because they know the law firm won't fight.

What you want to look for in a plaintiff's lawyer is whether he or she appears to be a person who can stand up before a judge and jury and fight for you. This is not a game for the timid. Plaintiffs' lawyers (and criminal-defense lawyers) are the toughest in the profession because they take on billion-dollar insurance companies and giant corporations who are capable of sending teams of lawyers to battle a big case.

A type of lawyer who does not work for you but who may represent you at some stage in your life is an insurance defense lawyer. If you are in an auto accident, or your child damages someone else's property, a lawyer who works directly for the insurance company (house counsel) or for a firm that probably devotes most of its practice for insurance companies, is assigned to you. I say "assigned" because even though the lawyer represents you in the matter, their true loyalty is to the insurance company who pays their bill. That doesn't mean they are necessarily going to screw you—but if it came to protecting your rights or that of the insurance company, who are they going to work the hardest for? Just keep that in mind when dealing with them.

Criminal-defense lawyers operate off a different fee basis than a plaintiff's lawyer—they get their money "up front" because that is the only way they will get paid. Considering that over 90 percent of their clients end up getting convicted for something, if they don't get paid up front, they won't get paid at all. *A good criminal-defense lawyer is a pit bull with a brain.* This is not a field for the timid—prosecutors eat the timid alive. They know when they are up against an attorney who is bluffing about going to trial and one that will drive them crazy and put them through a long trial if they don't offer a good deal. Because the criminal-justice system is so overwhelmed, hiring an attorney who a prosecutor knows is aggressive is a giant leap ahead. But make sure you are not just hiring a "dump truck." Many of these lawyers are full of sound and fury the day you hire them . . . and dump you on the day of trial when the hot air sizzles out.

When it comes to "winning" a criminal case, it rarely ends up with the defendant walking out of the courtroom (despite what you saw in the OJ trial). The vast majority of the cases are won in getting the defendant a plea to a reduced charge or lighter punishment. (Plea bargaining, despite the bad rap it gets in the press, is good for both sides—it permits prosecutors to get rid of cases that are hard to prove or are not worth the effort.)

Public defenders also have a bad press. The truth is that the average public defender is better able to handle the average case than a private lawyer. (Remember, more than 90 percent of defendants end up being found guilty.) Where they fail is in handling a tough case, and they fail for two reasons: (1) Most of them have such an excessive case load that they cannot put the time that a private attorney would put into the case, and (2) many public defenders have had their souls rotted by working in a bureaucracy and representing so many slimy bastards. (I can understand how they feel—I read fifty-two Perry Mason books as a kid and when I started handling criminal cases I thought all my clients were going to be beautiful women falsely accused of murdering their millionaire husband. What an awakening I got the first time I walked into a jail.)

You have to be more careful hiring a plaintiff's attorney (who works on a contingency) or a criminal-defense attorney (who is paid in full up front) than you do a business attorney, who is paid on an hourly basis. You can fire the business lawyer anytime along the line, although you may get into a situation in which you will have to pay another attorney to get up to speed on the case. Business litigation attorneys handle contractual disputes and actions between companies. What you should look for is not necessarily someone who is great in court (these cases are tried differently than criminal and personal-injury cases) but someone who is a smooth negotiator and who knows how to get rid of a case by settling it. Because these attorneys work on an hourly basis, some of them aren't motivated to resolve a case because the more problems there are, the more money they make. (After I pushed a case with over twenty attorneys on it into a settlement, one of the attorneys followed me out into the courthouse hallway and angrily accused me of costing him a quarter of a million dollars in fees.)

Before putting money into litigation, you should ask yourself whether it will be worth it. If a case can be settled, you can avoid tremendous headaches and huge expenses. Where people go wrong in business litigation is not analyzing their options. You get the options from your attorney, but remember that the lawyer has a conflict of interest because if the case doesn't settle, he or she earns more money. Good lawyers don't think that way, but there are plenty who do. Before you jump into litigation, find out whether settlement, mediation, or arbitration are viable alternatives. Or if just walking away from the problem is the right course—some things just aren't worth the hassle.

Many divorce lawyers are not at the top of my respect list. It isn't that they aren't doing a necessary job or that they don't earn their money—but divorces are generally not a positive thing and the more *un*positive the divorce gets, the more the lawyer earns. However, not all of them are in it for the money. I have found that there are generally two types of divorce lawyers: There are the socially sensitive ones who approach the job somewhat like marriage counselors and who deal with the person getting a divorce on a conscionable level, and then there are the sharks—these are the ones who put a dollar sign on every aspect of human misery and are out to get every buck that they can.

If there is a dispute over significant property, custody, or support, you should look for someone more aggressive than a marriage counselor and less of a rip-off than a shark. Divorce lawyers are expensive, but divorce fights over property (and sadly, too often over child custody) are a war, and you have to win the war. Think of it as two countries battling over the same territory. Someone is going to win, and someone is going to lose.

My remarks are premised on the fact there is a *dispute*. If you and your spouse are capable of sitting down and reasonably and logically dealing with the property and only need lawyers to memorialize the agreement, that's great. But that happens all too rarely. What is more common is that the hurt and pain of the separation causes one side or the other to strike out, and custody, support, and property division are the only areas where they can get in punches. There is also the greed factor—sometimes the other spouse just wants *more*.

Tough divorce lawyers who go into court and get you what you want earn their money. Socially conscious lawyers who guide you through the divorce and keep you from getting too emotionally scalped earn their money. Where the system goes astray is where a person is in so much pain and hurt that they just want to strike out at the other party and use the lawyers to do it. When that happens, the person has left themselves open to get financially ripped off by the lawyers and emotionally scarred in the whole process.

There are also lawyers known as transactional lawyers who do contracts and business agreements, probate lawyers who do wills and trusts, patent and intellectual-property lawyers, entertainment lawyers, and a host of others. Many work off an hourly fee.

When dealing with lawyers working on an hourly basis, get the agreement in writing—read the agreement and ask questions about it.

Business-type lawyers and others working off of an hourly fee have created a huge number of "hidden costs." When a lawyer charges you an hourly fee usually that is all you pay unless there are court costs or extraordinary expenses. But we are in an age of "law factories" in which it is not unusual for a law firm to have hundreds of lawyers and hundreds of staff and the firm is run as a business rather than a profession. With the law factories came sophisticated billing practices that the smaller firms picked up on. In addition to adding long-distance phone charges, many now have a telephone charge for local calls. (I'm not talking about the attorney time on the phone—I'm talking about a surcharge to the client for the attorney using *his own phone* for a local call and charging as if he was at a hotel!) Then they added photocopy charges—usually twenty to fifty times their actual cost per page. Then charges for "word processing." And paralegals. And assistants. And file storage. And etc., etc.

What exactly is the hourly fee for if it isn't to cover most of these items? I can see charging for making a large number of copies—and sending them to a copy company who does it for a fraction of the charge. But most of this is pure gouging. I've noticed that even some plaintiffs' lawyers have added this to their contingency fee contracts so they can do some gouging when the case settles.

Another scam, and every major corporation in America falls for it, is what I call the "senior partner" routine. Junior associate at the firm writes a letter and sends it to the opposition. The associate also "sends" it to the partner in the office next door that she or he reports to. That partner sends it to the senior partner down the hall who is in charge of the unit that associate and partner are in. One letter. One lawyer bills for writing it. Two other lawyers get to bill for reading it. And that's just at this law firm. The same routine goes on at the firm that received the letter. While some letters may be that important, this is usually simply a rip-off.

I have done plaintiff's work and often joked with my clients that we would settle the case after the lawyers opposing us got a full belly—i.e., after they have sucked all the fees that they can from the case.

Before we leave this subject, I am going to give you one more example of how we make victims of ourselves. This happened a long time ago, when I was a brand-new lawyer in a small town. The woman who walked into my office was one of my first clients.

I was desperate for clients and eager to get into court and be a champion for the downtrodden, and she fit the bill—except that she didn't have any money. I mean zero. She told me that her husband owned a convenience store on the outskirts of town and had considerable real estate. That made him well-off, in fact rather affluent for the area. As I listened to physical and mental abuse she went through at this bastard's hands, I was outraged. He had thrown her out of the house—physically—left her without money and moved another woman into the house to mother her children. Let's call her Mrs. Jones (this was before the days of "Ms.").

She was a match made in heaven for me. Lawyers don't have a choice in whom they represent, but I was determined to be the champion of the underdog. This was in the first couple of months of my law practice and I was also pretty desperate to generate cases and money. The only cases that I had dealt with up to that time had been a woman who had been thrown out of her last lawyer's office and spit on (I'm serious) and a kid charged with a petty offense. I got the kid off with a small fine and was so wound up because he couldn't pay the fine and would have to do a weekend in jail (I imagined him being beaten by guards and gang-raped by his cellmates) that I paid his fine on his promise that he would go home and get the money and come to my office with it. Which, of course, he never did.

The fact that the woman in my office didn't have money was not that significant. Her husband had money, and the way divorces work, the one with the money pays the lawyers for both sides. Besides, it wasn't just a question of money—I could fight for a good cause.

She didn't even have the money to pay for the filing fee for the divorce. I didn't have the money to spare but if I didn't pay it she'd never see her kids, so I prepared the papers, typing them up as she fed me the information (I didn't have a secretary yet), and took them down to the courthouse and filed them, paying the filing fee myself. In those days we had a process where upon good cause you could immediately get court orders affecting custody of children and occupancy of the family home without even notifying the other party, especially if you represented the wife, because men were almost always excluded from the home. I got a judge to sign the temporary orders and then had to figure out how I would get them served.

It's customary to have legal papers served by a process server, but the woman had no money, and I would have had to pay, so I thought, what the hell, I'd take the papers out to the guy's store myself and drop them off. I wasn't real enthused about doing it because I had heard horror stories of people lashing out at lawyers and process servers in divorce cases. (Many years later, after I had moved on to a big city, the divorce attorney who took over my office was murdered by an irate person who walked into the office and shot him.)

I drove to the convenience store and went in. There was a man about forty years old behind the counter. I asked for Mr. Jones, he said that was him, and I slapped the papers on the counter, and said, "These are for you." I quickly left the store and was pulling out of the parking lot when he came running out of the store. My heart was pounding as he came up to my car window because I was sure he was going to punch me out.

"She isn't my wife," he told me.

It seemed that a few months ago "Mrs. Jones" had come into his store to make a purchase. They engaged in some small talk and then she left the store. That night when he closed up and went to his car she was sitting in his car. When he asked her what she was doing in his car, she told him, "It's our car, darling."

This began a nightmare for him. She came to his house and tried to throw out his wife, claiming the children were hers. He had her arrested and a restraining order issued, but it didn't do any good. She had a fixation that she was married to him.

I was the third lawyer who had filed a divorce for her.

I went back to the office devastated and defeated. I not only was out time and money (time I had but the money really hurt), but I was humiliated at having been fooled. I tried to call her and discovered it was a disconnected number. The only address I had for her was the Jones house, and I wasn't going to look for her there. . . .

A couple of months went by before I got a call from her from a hospital. She told me Mr. Jones was her husband and had beaten the crap out of her. I was between a rock and a hard spot—I didn't want to fall for any more of her stories, but it was possible Mr. Jones had put one over on me and I had left her to his mercy.

At the hospital they told me that she was in something called the "crisis ward." I waited outside the ward for a nurse to let her know I was there. I heard the doors swing open behind me and turned as she came into the corridor. She was wearing a white hospital gown. There were no marks on her face but her eyes were a little wild and her hair was standing straight up as if she had been electrocuted.

She walked up to me and said, "Take me out of here, darling."

I don't know how long I stood there foolishly gaping at her. I don't even remember what I said in reply.

The moral to this story is that I was a victim waiting to happen. I was so eager to help that I didn't take ordinary precautions in dealing with a strange woman who walked into my office. I never saw her or heard from her again. I don't know if she ever recovered or left the hospital.

There is an old joke that has a moral for all of us when it comes to dealing with lawyers: When a forty-year-old lawyer was being interviewed by St. Peter at the gates to heaven, St. Peter was surprised at how young the lawyer was. From his hourly billing records, St. Peter had expected a one-hundred-year-old man.

PART III

Protecting Your Life and Home

Television has brought back murder into the home—where it belongs.

—Alfred Hitchcock

13

Getting Street-Smart

The idea that crime is "random" is a dangerous fallacy. Criminals are opportunists, and we create the opportunities for them to victimize us. People who maintain an awareness of the conditions around them and have good security habits are taking into consideration the risks of crime and reducing the probabilities of being a victim. Thinking about risks before putting your life on the line is the essence of being street-smart. It's learned behavior, and we can learn from example.

One night when I was a teenager my car broke down near a gas station. My mother was in the car with me, and we got out and went to the pay telephone at the gas station to call home. In those days we were always broke, and that night we only had loose change between us. My mother never owned or drove an automobile and didn't have a high tolerance level for things mechanical—she had a powerful personality, and I think she just couldn't stand not being able to force a car on empty to keep moving down the road or a telephone to refuse to operate at her command. That night she managed to lose a couple of dimes in the phone (a dime was the price of a call back then), the last money we had on us, and she flew into a rage, smashing the receiver against the rest of the pay phone.

The gas-station attendant started toward us, yelling out that he was going to call the police. My mother snarled back, "Good, go ahead. And when they get here I'm going to tell them you raped me."

He spun around and went back into the station.

I will admit that smashing pay phones and intimidating gas-station attendants do not rank high in any of our estimates of civilized human behavior . . . but my mother was a woman who had to deal with a deadbeat husband and raise a houseful of kids with her wits. She didn't learn how to handle people at an MBA program at Harvard. More importantly, from my earliest memories to when she died in my twenties, I never saw her lose control of a situation. Whether it was sweet-talking a motel clerk out of a room because we were stranded on the road or talking a boss into giving her a job, she had a skill for dealing with people.

A few months after she died I found myself in the middle of the street on a dark night in a big city with a crazy shoving a gun into my gut. I know my mother put the words into my mouth that kept me alive that night.

Our reactions to everyday situations are a product of life-long conditioning. Too many of us have been raised in a social womb that takes care of us until we are ready to leave the nest. Most people over forty years old were raised in a society in which crime was not at epidemic levels. The crime plague started in the 1960s with the advent of widespread drug use in our culture and continued an almost vertical rise into the 1990s as we lost the war on drugs and a generation of drug-fried crazies took over our streets.

A categorical imperative for all of us is to survive the

plague of crime by taking control of our own safety. To do this we have to break the mode and get rid of bad "security" habits that give criminals the opportunities to make us victims.

A popular fallacy about crime is that it is random, that it only happens to us when we are in the wrong place at the wrong time. That is true in some cases, but there are two things wrong with the premise: (1) most victims created the wrong place and time. Criminals are opportunists and we create the opportunity—if we are in a bank in broad daylight and robbers come in, that is random crime; but when we go to bed with the bathroom window unlocked, when we go to an ATM machine at night or drop by a convenience store for a quart of milk after a movie, we have just put ourselves into the wrong place at the wrong time because all of these activities involve a high degree of risk. And, (2) because we are under the false belief that crime is simply random, we disarm ourselves from a security standpoint because "there's nothing we can do about it."

Knowing how to take control of your personal safety, how to be prepared to protect yourself and your loved ones from crime, and what to do when your best-laid plans all go to hell and you are in a tight spot, all relate to being *street-smart*—even when you are using the "smarts" to protect yourself in your home, at a motel while traveling, or while on the job.

Since most of us have been raised in a secured cocoon and are live bait for criminals, to step out of the victim mode and get control over our personal safety we have to break the mode just as we have had to deal with other bad habits, or face the consequences. People are naturally resistant to change, but we can change if we are motivated.

The steps set out below all relate to our *state of mind* because that's where being security smart begins and ends. Either you want to be security conscious or you don't. If you do, you have to get rid of some bad habits and get yourself thinking about things you never thought of before—or in ways you never thought of them.

In the following chapters detailed procedures for *implementing* the steps with security measures are laid out—making your home safe, tips on security when driving, jogging, going out to dinner, movies, traveling, at work and other situations.

The steps put you into the right frame of mind to get security smart, and the detailed security measures tell you how to accomplish it.

Be Aware of Your Surroundings

Many people stumble through life oblivious to everything around them. The most important step in being street-smart is to develop an awareness that you can become a victim. If you are the average person, you have more awareness of the foods that keep you healthy and how to protect your car than you have of protecting your life and those of your loved ones.

Most crime victims have placed themselves in jeopardy by not giving thought to where they park their car, the locking devices on their doors and windows at home, when and where they shop, and a host of other small matters that often turn into big problems. They make almost *every place* they go the *wrong* place and *wrong* time.

When we step outside our home, to keep from being a victim we have to maintain an awareness of our environment rather than being mindless.

Two concepts need to be emphasized:

- *That personal safety deserves as much thought and attention in our life as the car we drive, what goes in our stomach, and the TV shows we watch.*
- *That there is something we can do to survive the plague of crime on our streets.*

Once we develop a consistent awareness of our surroundings, we can reduce even the random chance of being the victim of crime by taking some basic steps. More important, we can stop creating the wrong-place and wrong-time scenario that creates opportunities for criminals and sends our chances of being a victim sky-high.

Get Automatic

When you start *thinking* about security, forming good security habits becomes easy. The essence of the victim mentality is that it is an unconscious bad habit that even the best and sharpest people have. People don't put themselves in danger because they have thought about it—they have done so because they didn't give personal safety enough thought.

We already have been trained in some habits—we look before we cross the street, put on our seat belt when we get in our car, and lock our residence door at night.

We need to *expand* our security awareness and turn that awareness into a daily routine, forming *habits that will protect our life no matter where we are.*

We form good security habits by simply doing the technique until it becomes *automatic*. (Remember what they told you in school—*repetition* is the mother of learning.)

For example, most people drive cars at some point in

their life. Safe people lock their car doors when they get in. In fact, many new cars come equipped with automatic door locks that lock as soon as you turn on the key. There is no question that locking your car doors is a good safety and security habit. *But almost everyone locks them too late.*

I have a habit of locking my car door as I am stepping into the car. By the time the door swings shut, all the doors are locked. We are at risk when we get to our car and open the door. But the faster we lock our doors, the more chance we have of avoiding someone jumping in and putting a knife to our throat.

It doesn't take any more effort to lock the door *when* we are getting in than it does to lock it *after* we get in. By getting into the *habit* of locking our doors quickly we reduce our chances of being a victim because it is at the moment we are distracted getting into our car that we are most vulnerable to being attacked.

I don't do it because I am paranoid—I don't even think about it. It is simply an automatic response to getting in a car, a safety habit I have formed after dealing with a criminal who told me that he timed his attack on a woman in a parking lot to when she had already unlocked the doors to her car and before getting fully settled into the driver's seat. He jumped into the car on the passenger side and he would have been too late had she locked the door seconds earlier. He chose getting into the car with her because had he accosted her in the open, she might have attracted attention with a scream and tried to run.

It doesn't cost me anything to lock my doors when I am getting in. Even if I didn't have automatic door locks, I could hit the door lock on my way in. It doesn't take any more time. And it's making the long shot of being a victim in a parking lot a *very* long shot. But only because it's an automatic response that I do without thinking. If I had to think about it, I probably wouldn't remember to do it very often.

Be Prepared

Being suddenly confronted with violent crime in which we are the intended victim may be the biggest crisis any of us will go through in our lives. Being prepared is fundamental to dealing with any crisis.

Don't ever underestimate the power of being prepared mentally.

If you believe that you can't be prepared for random acts of crime—you're wrong. Maybe dead wrong.

Pointed out in another section is that most people believe they have absolutely no control over surviving a plane crash—thus do nothing to prepare. Yet US government studies show that people who prepare themselves for a crash by *thinking out* what they would do in the event of such an emergency have a higher survival rate than the passengers who never give it a thought. When the emergency occurred and others sat stunned, persons who were prepared reacted *immediately* to save their own lives.

Getting confronted by a criminal act can't be any more shocking than suddenly finding yourself in a crashing plane.

Some preparation is "preventive" maintenance—buying easy-to-install security hardware for our windows and doors, a panic button at bedside, and the many more commercial and homespun security devices mentioned in this book.

But most preparation is mental. All the hardware and mechanical devices in the world may not help if we do not maintain a security-conscious state of mind. Being prepared mentally is the easy part—you will get there just by reading about it and giving it a little thought. We don't have to go lie down in the freeway to see if we can roll out of the way of the trucks to get prepared to handle a crisis. We can read about it, think about it, and develop a state of mind that will kick in when the crisis erupts.

People caught up in the victim mentality don't give thought to how they will handle a criminal act before it occurs. Some people carry this same mentality into everything they do. They don't have a contingency plan for anything. Things just happen, and they are the ones it happens to the most frequently. Some things simply can't be ignored. Being able to change a tire on a car if you get a flat is a contingency plan for that emergency. Many people, especially women, don't know how to do this simple function safely. And sadly, a number of the women who have been kidnapped by crazies had the misfortune to have a flat tire and turn an otherwise simple drive into a nightmare.

If you are the type who things simply "happen" to, keep this rather crude street expression in mind: *Shit happens.*

This is a tough world. It's a complicated one. It's too damn much for most of us, and we have to struggle just to survive. Don't make it harder on yourself by not giving thought to your own personal safety and that of the people you love.

Avoid Dangerous Mind-Sets

A mind-set is a frame of mind that causes us to do something without giving it any thought. Mental sets can be dangerous because they are holes in our security state of mind. They are not just bad habits but ways in which we have fooled ourselves into lapsing into the victim mentality.

For example, take working for a company and parking in the employee parking lot. We don't give parking there any thought because it's just taken for granted that it is safe because we have parked there hundreds of times and it's a company lot. It's as if we are immune from danger because it is a *company* lot. But let's say you work late one night. *Break the mental set*—people get murdered and raped in employee parking lots just the same as they do in supermarket and mall lots. If you are going to work late, take a break while it's still daylight and move your car to as secure a location as you can—and if there are any other employees around when it is time to leave, ask them to watch you go to your car.

The employee parking lot is only one example. Life is full of these mental sets. It will be pointed out later that one of the most highly publicized attacks of the 1990s occurred because the victim was driving in a high crime area without the vehicle doors locked—most likely because it was a *company* vehicle.

People fall into these mind-sets wherever they go. They act as if the clerk in the twenty-four-hour market they stop at to get a quart of milk late at night is going to be able to handle the drug-crazed nuts with Saturday Night Specials who pick up the money for their next fix at these places. They get on a plane and assume that the 120-pound flight attendant is going to smile professionally and point out the exits as the plane is sliding on its belly and bursting into flames on the runway. They gorge themselves with popcorn in a movie theater, their eyes glued to the action on the screen, and never once does their eye stray to locate which side of the theater the exit is. In case of fire, with hundreds of people stampeding and the theater cloaked in darkness, they expect the popcorn attendant to guide them out.

These examples may be a bit exaggerated, but I present them to drill home the point: Don't get into a mental set that you are safe because someone else is in charge of your safety. *You are in charge.*

Don't Fall into the Dominant-Person Trap

If you live with someone, it is probable that each of you contributes to the relationship and the household chores in slightly different ways, with one person dominating certain chores. For example, while this may sound like a stereotype, in our society women tend to be the dominant person in parenting, men tend to be the dominant person in regard to caring for the family car.

There should be no dominant person in regard to security.

Every one in the household has to take a hand in security, or the household will never be consistently secure. One person cannot be running from room to room checking windows and doors. And one person can't be in the household twenty-four hours a day, seven days a week to make sure everything is secure.

Keep in mind that most criminals do not come through the front door with a battering ram. They most frequently enter through unlocked or poorly secured windows and doors. The highly publicized, tragic rape-murder of the little girl at a slumber party came about that way.

Having all the greatest security hardware in the world won't help if someone in the household leaves the bathroom window open. That scenario will occur most frequently when everyone in the household fails to take responsibility for family security.

The most dangerous mind-set that people have is that there is someone other than themselves who is responsible for their personal safety. The police, spouse, lover, parents, none of these people are your shadow. The police won't be there when danger strikes. Your loved ones are just another set of victims for someone higher on the food chain to eat.

Don't get into that fatal mind-set that someone else will do it for you, someone else will be responsible for the bathroom window, locking the car doors, or double-locking the motel room, because that someone else either won't be around or won't be any help when danger strikes.

You are the dominant person in your life when it comes to personal safety because you are the only one that is always going to be there and might just be the only one who always cares.

Be Responsible for Your Own Life

Birth and death are a lonely business even if you have friends and family at your side. They can share the moment but not the pain. You came in alone and you're going to leave alone. You are responsible for your actions while you're aboard. Take control and responsibility for your own life.

I pointed out that people get into mental sets and relationships in which they turn over running their lives to others or rely upon others for help in situations in which helpers cannot perform even if they wanted to. Too many people even sheepishly trust their lives to strangers without giving it any thought. Children are led away from shopping malls to horrors because they trust the pervert that takes them by the hand. Women are brutalized because they turn their head and an acquaintance dumps a date-rape drug in their drink. Naive people are lured into danger or out of their money by hustlers on the Internet.

We naturally trust other people, and there is no reason why we shouldn't. Most people are decent. But we have to give some thought to where and when to draw the line. An incredible amount of crime in this country occurs because we are too trusting . . . serial killer Ted Bundy oozed trust-worthiness to the several dozen women he murdered.

Sometimes we fall into what I call *institutionalized* trust. Nothing can happen to us because we have put our trust in another entity. The mind-set revealed in the company-car and employee-parking-lot scenarios are examples. The motel situation mentioned earlier is another example of institutional trust. We check into a motel and get into a mental set of trust that somehow the motel itself is a sort of security blanket (when the truth is many motels are high crime areas in and of themselves, and the people working there are no better at taking care of their own safety than we are).

Security-conscious people do not assume that a night clerk is going to provide them with security. There are other actions they take. For example, when they check in, they ask for a second-floor room. They check the windows. They set up a "room invasion" alarm from items in their own toiletries. (Before you assume I am joking, take a look at the traveling safely chapter—most of the security habits I practice when traveling are recommended by the US State Department for its personnel.)

This theme about giving a little thought about who we are going to trust with our life needs to be repeated over and over until it becomes automatic with us. *You don't trust your life to other people.* I'm not talking about fire or police personnel. I'm talking about institutional-type trust, that someone else is in charge and will be responsible for our safety. Don't bet that there will be a hotel bellperson in the hallway at the time a nasty bastard who had your room the day before comes back with a key to rape you. I have dealt with the exact situation with a victim.

Develop a "Speak-Softly" Attitude

Remember the advice Teddy Roosevelt gave: "Speak softly and carry a big stick."

That was good advice in Roosevelt's day, the turn of the century when America was a wild and woolly place, and it's good advice now that our streets have some of the less desirable attributes of the Old West.

The most important "big stick" I know of in regard to personal security is *attitude.*

Some people are simply shark bait—criminals take one look at them and hone in. A friend of mine claims that he can walk down the meanest streets of the cities and no one would touch him because of the aura of confidence he displays. (Personally I think no one would touch him because they would be laughing too hard.) But there is some truth to the theory. If you act like a victim, if you look like a victim, you are probably going to become a victim.

Who is a criminal going to come after—the person who wanders around oblivious to everything going on, or someone who appears to be looking out for themselves.

That doesn't mean that crime only knocks on the door of the timid. Part of attitude, a very major part, is not to be macho. If you sense a dangerous situation, don't like the looks of someone or a street or even getting on an elevator, turn on your heel and avoid the situation.

Attitude is all about avoiding trouble and moving expediently to get out of it once you've stepped in it.

Crime finds all of us sometime or other. But the person who is going to have the best chance of surviving is the person with the right attitude. Sometimes that attitude is a matter of showing confidence. Other times it is simply knowing when to keep your mouth shut or when to scream and yell for help.

In terms of personal security I believe in going quietly about my business. I try not to be pushy. But when the chips are down and my life is in danger, I will take out all stops.

Speak softly . . . walk quietly . . . don't go looking for trouble. But when trouble finds you, make sure you are prepared for it with your attitude.

I am going to take you through dozens of different situations from around the house and mall, to around the world. The situations are all different but the formula for dealing with them is always the same: to develop good habits that will lead you through most of the emergencies you will face. Some life-threatening situations are obviously not in our control—we can't carry a parachute aboard a 747 in case it does a nose dive from 40,000 feet. But that doesn't mean we turn over all of safety concerns about flying to an anonymous ticket order taker on the telephone. As you will see in the section on air travel, there are many things that we can do to increase our chances of avoiding an air disaster or surviving one if it occurs.

We will fall back on these "street-smart—security-smart" attributes over and over to deal with the hundreds of different situations encountered.

When being security conscious becomes second nature, you will be better prepared to handle and survive almost any situation.

Keep also in mind that life is very much a game of chance. The "odds" are being played in your life from the moment of conception when your propensity for everything from competing at the Olympics to your ability to get certain types of cancer are being inbred.

You can get wiped out on the freeway tomorrow or stepping out of your bathtub due to bad luck. I have friends who carry this fatalistic mentality to the point that they don't even wear a seat belt in a car because they figure when it's time to go, they go. What they don't realize is that they may go a little faster than the rest of us.

If I told you that I could show you a way to save $2 but that you would have to take a million to one long shot that it would cost you your life, you probably would tell me to shove off. It's a ridiculous offer. But when you go to an exposed ATM at night instead of going to an inside ATM in a store where you might have to pay a dollar or two for the use of the ATM, but where there is no danger, you have just taken a long shot on your life for a couple of bucks.

We make these sort of *Dollars vs. Life* decisions frequently. Every day of the year, someone in a big city returning home late at night on a subway from a movie and dinner is being mugged or killed. It is a million to one long shot of it happening to you. But when you make that decision to save $10 on taxi fare, you have just made a *Dollars vs. Life* decision.

The same sort of decision-making, risk-taking process is involved when you ignore valet parking in front of a restaurant and park on a side street, when you save $15 or $20 on a motel room that is just a little less secure than the one down the street, when you choose a discount airline which uses older equipment than standard airlines, when you save $10 a day but take a subcompact rental car that would not survive a collision with a squirrel. . . .

Unless you are independently wealthy, you have to make these *Dollars vs. Life* decisions. There is nothing wrong with making the decision—most of us couldn't go anywhere or do anything if it always had to be at the highest expense.

The issue isn't whether we should make such decisions but that we should make them *unconsciously*. We wouldn't risk our life *consciously* for peanuts, but we do it every day without thinking.

Now is the time to start thinking about it.

Thinking about risks before putting our life on the line is the essence of being street-smart.

14

Home Security

The high-crime area where we are the most vulnerable

Ladybug, ladybug, fly away home,
Your house is on fire, and your children will
burn.

—"Ladybug, Ladybug"

We have been coddled into a false sense of security in our homes without an awareness that the world has changed over the past couple of decades and that there are millions of drug-damaged criminals in our society. People go to sleep at night with the bathroom window unlatched or nothing but a screen between them and the darkness. There are nearly two million burglaries a year, and almost half of them occur at night. There are simple things we can do to make our homes more secure, basic items that each of us should have and contingency plans that each of us should know.

Remember the expression, the proud boast . . . my home is my castle? In olden days castles were built to protect the surrounding countryside against roaming marauders. Villagers built their homes close to the castle walls so they could run into the castle when danger threatened. We no longer have castle walls to protect us . . . not even "security apartment complexes" and gated housing developments afford much protection.

As businesses install security cameras, alarm systems, and hire guards, making them tougher for criminals to deal with, criminals are looking more and more to private homes as their source of income. And they have a partner-in-crime—the homeowner.

People who turn every place they go into the *wrong* place turn the place they spend the most time into the wrong place *all* of the time.

This is another one of those areas where the brightest and most successful people are the most gullible when it comes to taking care of security. Dynamic people who go to the office and jealously guard the assets of a business owned by someone else, take little care in protecting their own families and property.

According to the FBI, there are close to *two million* residential burglaries a year. About 59 percent of the burglaries occur in the daytime and 41 percent at night. It's logical that more home burglaries would occur in the daytime than at night because that is when people are at work and school, but what is surprising is that nearly half of the burglaries occur at night, when a greater percent of people would be home.

Two-thirds of the burglaries involved forced entry. That means that in one out of every three burglaries, the thieves do not even have to force their way in.

Isn't that a striking statistic: In one-third of the burglaries, six or seven hundred thousand burglaries a year, the homeowner has left a window or door unlocked to permit a thief in. And almost half of those thieves enter at night, when people are most likely to be in their homes. I wonder how many of those entries were made when the apartment or home dweller was asleep.

Can you guess what month most burglaries happen? The hottest month of the year—August. That seems natural because during the summer we would be inclined to leave windows open to let in a breeze. We lie down to sleep with that cool breeze coming in from the open window. At night. When there are hundreds of thousands of home burglaries a year and tens of thousands of rapes—at night, in home sweet home, our castle.

What's wrong with this picture? We just turned our home into the wrong place and wrong time. I had neighbors in a nice area murdered in their bed on a warm summer night because they opened the sliding glass door to their bedroom and left nothing between them and the bogeyman except a screen. Of course, not everyone gets murdered in their beds. There are also 100,000 forcible rapes reported a year. And a whole bunch more that never get reported.

I have a friend, a macho kind of guy, who lives in Malibu and prides himself on not locking the door at night (I have several friends scattered across the country who have this same fantasy, that it's safe to sleep in a house with unlocked doors and windows). This friend keeps a gun near the bed and he thinks that will keep him safe. We will go into guns in the home in a later chapter, but it should be obvious to anyone with any common sense that if just one of those two million residential burglaries occur at his house, someone might cut his throat before he has a chance to reach for that gun. Someone should also disabuse him of the misconception that there aren't any fewer drug-crazed nuts running around Malibu than anywhere else. The difference is that in Malibu some of the drug-crazed nuts earn ten million dollars a year acting in movies.

Of course my friend has two cars and a motorcycle. Kept locked. And alarmed.

Sleeping with the doors and windows unlocked in Malibu probably isn't any worse than my friend in a New York apartment who frequently leaves unlocked the steel mesh protecting entry from the fire escape because she forgets to lock it after watering plants. All of these people are potential victims who have created the opportunity for criminals to strike at them. What they don't appreciate is that they are throwing the dice with their lives in the pot.

Don't buy into this mentality. Whether you're in a run-down, inner-city apartment, a home in the burbs, or a farm in the country, there are things you should do to protect the lives of you and your family. Some of the things sound real simplistic: like keeping the doors and windows locked, especially after dark. But what we *think* we do, and what really happens, are often two different things.

The Dominant-Person Trap

Home security often suffers from the dominant-person trap: One person in the household is security conscious and makes sure the doors and windows are locked.

But when he or she is away from the home, all of the doors and windows don't get locked. Why? Because *only* one person is security conscious. No one operates at 100% capacity all of the time and when the security-conscious person is not around or forgets, the rest of the family doesn't pick up the slack.

Even worse, when a person who is not security conscious is off on their own, for an evening, a weekend, school, or a lifetime, this victim-waiting-to-happen will expose themselves and others to danger.

Unless everyone in the household is security conscious,

you will never create a secured household because there will be a weak link who will crack open a bathroom window to let out steam and then go to bed and forget it or close a bedroom window and forget to lock it.

Establishing a Safe and Sane Routine

All households operate off of rules and with routines, no matter how casual they seem to be—televisions go off at a certain time, people go to bed, and lights go out, generally in a routine manner. These are "rules" that people in the household accept (with maybe some rebellion from the younger set occasionally).

Household security must become a routine and rules set down even if you live alone and will be the only one following them.

The first rule is to get into the habit of making sure doors are kept locked all of the time and windows are locked definitely after dark and anytime you are not home. Windows that are out of sight, out of mind, should be kept locked even in the daytime. Note again that more than half of the home burglaries take place in the daytime.

Make sure everyone in the household follows the rule and gets used to the routine.

You are most vulnerable when you are asleep, so shouldn't you have the most security when you're asleep? Some security measures before sleeping should be SOP (Standard Operating Procedures): Get in the habit of double-checking all doors and windows. And get everyone in the household in the same habit, not just their own window and door, but all the household apertures. A good way to do this is to stagger the responsibility so everyone has the duty once in a while and the whole household ends up security conscious.

What is the significance of locking doors and windows? If someone wants in, they can kick in the door or break a window.

The point is exactly the one that those who ask this question are making, but it doesn't strike home with them because they are not security conscious and don't think the situation through to the end—doors and windows that are locked have to be kicked in or broken to gain entry—and that makes *noise*. What does your car alarm do? What does your home alarm do? Alarms make noise because noise is the best warning and best defense against crime (albeit, no one pays that much attention to a car alarm anymore).

By establishing a routine where doors and windows are kept secured, especially at night, and thus forcing a criminal to do something that will create noise, even if you are the only one that will hear it or react to it, you have at least done the minimum in getting your residence secured. If you have someone forcing their way in one door, you may have a chance to get out a window or another door, call 911, scream for neighbors, break a window to attract attention to your plight, or arm yourself.

Without that early-warning device you lose all of these options. And you have increased your statistical chances of becoming a crime statistic.

Let's go back and play the *Dollars vs. Life* game, only this time we don't even have to ante up. It doesn't cost anything except a few seconds of your time to make sure that your doors and windows are secure. But once you have done it, you have increased your odds of surviving.

And there is one other factor that seems to be lost with my macho friends: What exactly is the point about sleeping with doors and windows unlocked? Is there something they have gained in return for the risk they have taken to their lives? If you go to the ATM machine at night because you don't want to pay the store ATM the gain to use their machine, at least you save two dollars.

But what do these people gain?

The importance of *noise* needs to be emphasized: (a) the greatest fear home invaders have is noise that will warn the occupants or the neighbors, and you have now made it necessary for an intruder to make noise to get in; and (b) you and your loved ones have started on the road of being security conscious, a frame of mind that will follow you out onto the streets and perhaps save your life.

But locking up is only the *minimum*. You need to take more steps to protect your life.

Making It Hard to Get In

Locking any door or window makes it harder to get in, but there are locks . . . and there are *locks*.

Most windows need locking devices in addition to those that came from the factory. Factory locks are typically not security locks. Sliding aluminum-framed windows are ridiculously easy to force open from the outside. Often these windows can be removed in their entirety by someone standing outside.

Hardware stores and general-merchandise stores carry snap-on and screw-on locking devices that prevent someone from easily opening or removing sliding windows. If everything else fails, cut the end off old brooms or mops or pick up some dowels (round lengths of wood) at a lumber store and stick them in the window track.

Roll-out windows generally have additional latches and are usually the most difficult for a thief to access.

Wood-framed, lift-up windows are also high on the scale of security when they are kept locked.

Louvered windows are among the easiest to open from outside. But there is a simple metal catch that anyone can attach to make louvered windows nearly impossible to open from the outside without breaking them.

Sliding glass doors should get the same treatment as windows. Next to windows, this type of door is usually the easiest access into a house and the most often left unlocked. Even locked, they provide little protection unless double-locked. Broom handles work, but are not as effective as the locking devices sold specifically for them. You can also use these locking devices to leave the door open enough to let in some air or for a pet to go in and out and still have the door secure. At least that is the theory. But these doors are so easy to shift in the frame, I don't buy that theory. I know many people who leave their doors like this while they are at work for Fido to go in and out. If nothing else, the sight of a door cocked open six inches is an invitation to a thief to try some other way of getting in.

The idea behind adding a few dollars worth of hardware to your glass doors and windows is to make the intruder break it to get in. As long as you have warning, while they're coming in the back window, you can be running out the front screaming your head off.

Does locking windows prevent someone from getting in? Not someone who is so determined that they break the window, but few home invaders want to make that kind of noise if it warns the occupants or the neighbors might hear. The average intruder who would break into a residence is a drugged-out crazy or neighborhood teenager who is unlikely even to have a glass cutter—and glass cutters make noise.

Most doors are not much harder to break into than windows, especially back doors even if they have multiple locks. There is a fallacy about locks because no matter how strong your lock is, or how many locks you have, a door can often be kicked open with the strong locks left in place (i.e., the wood breaks while the lock stays in place). That is not to say that you should not have multiple locks in some situations—if nothing else, breaking a door with multiple locks may make more noise.

Front doors tend to be thicker and have more solid locks than back doors. Back doors are not only usually flimsy, but many back doors are partially glass, French doors, sliding glass, or the like. Sliding doors with glass are easier to break in than wooden doors with dead bolts unless you have the additional locks that keep these doors from being lifted out of their tracks or the locking device bent back. Glass is also a good noisemaker, so an intruder rarely will walk up and kick down a glass door.

A good dead bolt on front doors is usually sufficient. It won't keep someone from kicking it in, but here again, you cannot protect from every possible eventuality, and the odds are greater that someone would try to enter a back window than kick open a front door and risk alerting neighbors.

Good protection is provided by steel security screen doors. They are not always the prettiest trim on a house or apartment, but you can't kick them in, and they make it reasonably safe at night to open to someone who knocks.

Another device is a latch that prevents the door from being opened except from the inside. Those half-moon-shaped brass plates that are screwed into the frame and are slipped over the door work great. They also put up a bit more resistance to someone trying to kick your door open.

Any door with glass should have double-sided, keyed locks (a lock that takes a key to open even from inside) rather than the typical dead bolt that has a handle on the inside. This prevents someone from breaking the glass and reaching in to unlock the door. This isn't always convenient because the keys get lost and stolen, but being murdered can also ruin your whole day.

A necessary security device for the front door is a good peephole. Most doors have those little brass cylinders with magnified glass on the end. There are two things wrong with them: they are usually too small to see anyone except for a person standing directly in front of the peephole, and they don't allow you to speak to the person outside. There are larger versions of these cylinders and larger peepholes (a few inches square) that allow you to open a little door and speak to the person outside. This is safer than opening the door to speak to a stranger.

Don't have the tools (a hand drill) to put in a decent peephole in your door? No friends or relatives to help? Then pick up your local paper and call a handyman, who will do it for fifty bucks. Hell, if it was something for your car stereo, you'd spend more than that in a flash.

Should you open your door to a stranger at night? Is that opening the door to trouble? Why take the chance? And if you are a macho kind of guy or gal and don't scare easily, why risk your loved ones by opening the door to potential trouble?

What about all the good people who come around collecting for charities and selling honest products?

If you feel the need to give, tell them to leave the information in your mailbox or on your front porch and you'll send a check later. Tell them anything you like, but don't open the door.

How to avoid opening the door without shouting through it is where the enlarged peephole comes in. Other alternatives: If you have a window near the door, open the window enough to talk to the person at the door, or buy an inexpensive battery-operated "intercom" (a two-position intercom can be picked up at discount electronics stores for under $25); screw one end outside near the doorbell and the other inside near the door.

What do you do when someone runs up to your door and says they need your phone to call 911 for the police, ambulance, or fire department? A tow truck? You don't need to let them in the house to use your phone. You can dial the number for them.

This falls under the concept of not letting someone trick you into letting them into your home. Your home is your castle—don't let down the drawbridge and invite trouble in.

Home Security Checklist

1. Check each of your windows. If there is only the factory-installed lock, purchase easily installed window locks that you can remove with your fingers from the inside to open the window, but will trip up someone trying to open the window from the outside.

    These locks are inexpensive and are available at hardware and many general-merchandise stores. They are available for almost any type of window—sliding, louver, or wood-framed. Putting a stick in the path of a sliding window helps, but it is not as effective as the hardware.
2. Check all sliding doors. Install similar hardware that is used on sliding windows.
3. Doors with glass should have double-sided keyed locks as opposed to the standard dead bolt. That permits someone from breaking just enough glass to stick their hand through and turn the inside lock.

4. Check all doors that have outside access.
   a. You should have a "wide angle" peephole large enough to see a significant area in front of the door and that you can communicate through. An alternative to communicating through a peephole is a cheap intercom.
   b. All doors to the outside should have dead bolts.
   c. All doors to the outside should have a heavy-chain-type or other type of backup lock. The typical chain that you use to open a door to peek out when there is someone at your door is a joke and provides no real security.
   d. I personally prefer a "noisemaker" on door and windows. You can provide this with a professionally installed alarm system, a do-it-yourself system or even the battery-operated units that are for one door, one window, etc. The idea, whether you are in the suburbs or a high-rise big-city apartment, is to generate enough noise in an emergency to alert neighbors who will call the police.
   e. If you can't afford a real video camera, consider a "mock" video camera in the eaves of your roof over your front door. Get one that looks real.
   f. Consider alarm-on-premises window stickers and signs out front. Sometimes the sign alone is a deterrent. (Personally, I hate bluffing, especially when some crazy

with a gun calls your bluff—I suggest you really have an alarm to go with the signs.)

5. Establish a security routine that each member of the household complies with. This means checking windows and doors to ensure they are locked and that the added security devices are in place.

6. Speak to your neighbors and make a commitment to call the police if anyone hears anything suspicious. If you don't know your neighbors, this is a good time to meet them. If you are too shy, do a simple letter and put it in their mailboxes.

7. Homes with a yard should:
   a. Have a sliding bolt lock on the side gate low enough on the gate so that it cannot be reached by an intruder. The pull-string latch most of these gates are equipped with provide no security.
   b. Have outside sensor lighting. These are security lights that go on when motions are detected around the house. They are a wonderful security device because as an intruder walks up to the house, they are suddenly bathed in floodlights.
   c. Have ladders and other items in storage if intruders can use them to reach a second-story window or deck.
   d. Have a security screen door if it is inevitable that you or someone in your family will open the front door to strangers.

8. If you have a garage:
   a. Have an automatic garage-door opener, if possible. It permits you to drive your car

in without leaving the car and operates as a "lock" on the door.

   b. Secure the side door well to your garage if you have a typically flimsy door. These side doors are a prime way to get into a house because once someone is in your garage, they generally can gain easier and less noticeable access to your house than from the outside.

9. When your residence will be vacant for a night or more, because you are away, use a timer to turn on and off lights in one or two rooms at appropriate times. These timers can be picked up at hardware stores and discount stores.

10. Keep a flashlight next to the bed. This is a great emergency device for everything from home invasions to power outages. I prefer a policeman's type flashlight—an instrument about fifteen to twenty inches long that works nicely as a club if you need it.

11. Keep a small-to-medium-size fire extinguisher by your bed. Besides helping with a fire, they are great for spraying an intruder's face (if you can't run! if the slime doesn't have a gun! and a lot of other ifs!).

12. If you live too high up to jump in case of a fire, keep a gas mask and a coil of climbers rope under your bed. (Think I'm kidding? Maybe I am. But it is a thought, isn't it?)

13. Don't open your door to strangers. If they need a phone to call 911, do it for them. If they're with a charity organization, have them leave the material at your door or in your mailbox.

15

Security Systems

What were all the world's alarms
To mighty Paris when he found
Sleep upon a golden bed
That first night in Helen's arms?

—W. B. Yeats

Security systems are so cheap no home or apartment should be without one. Big-city apartment dwellers with six locks on their doors would be better served with a do-it-yourself alarm system that includes a bedside "panic button."

Noise, Noise, Noise

What is the big deal about an alarm system? It is a *noisemaker.*

Noise scares off most intruders before they are at your throat.

Noise is an early-warning device that lets you know that someone is about to be at your throat.

Noise warns everyone in the house—if you are not alone at least someone might get away to get help.

Noise can alert neighbors of your danger.

A system linked to a monitoring service usually costs less than dinner out for two once a month and will alert others—professionals who call the police—that you are in danger.

Let's take a look at home-security systems.

It's no longer necessary to have an expensive security alarm. A security system for a home or apartment can be picked up for a couple hundred dollars at your local discount electronics store. The do-it-yourself varieties are not that much more complicated to install than a stereo system with a couple of speakers.

Even the hard-wired, professionally installed variety cost a fraction of what they cost just a few years ago. You can usually have a system professionally installed that would alarm most apartments and modest-sized homes for less than what you would pay for a good sound system for your car.

Many of the systems come with a "panic" button that you keep by your bedside (or on your key ring) and can send off the alarm from inside or a reasonable distance outside.

As I mentioned before, I am amazed at how so many people spend the money to protect their fifteen-thousand-dollar car with an alarm system . . . but are too cheap or too naive to spend about the same amount of money to protect their life.

Security systems, even just the *signs* that go with security systems, are a tremendous deterrent to crime.

If you were a home invader, whose residence would you choose? Probably not the one with solid locks on doors and windows—and the house or apartment with signs indicating that the place is alarmed is going to be last on your list.

A living, breathing security alarm is the common household mutt—if it's a barker. While a barking dog will not win you popularity contests at an apartment complex, a mutt that gets excited and barks at every noise is an early-warning device that would scare off many home invaders.

If you are not into dogs, or in an apartment building where the neighbors will go ballistic over a barking dog, get an alarm system. (In this age of quality medical services for pets and designer dog foods, an alarm system will be cheaper in the long run but won't keep your feet warm on long winter nights.)

Police sometimes consider it a tip-off that someone you know burglarized your home when the burglar ignores your dog. Prime candidates for committing home burglaries are young people in the neighborhood who have been visitors in the victim's home and know the family's schedule, the layout of the home, and the temperament of the family dog. These thieves are the hardest to protect against because they may even have learned your alarm code by watching your children turn it off. This is a good reason to occasionally change your alarm code.

Another good reason to change your alarm code is that the crew that installed the alarm knows it.

Most people who are not security conscious are people who have never had anything happen to them. I have friends who live in a nice suburb of Salt Lake City and they and their neighbors pride themselves, like my Malibu friend, on not locking their doors at night or when they leave the house.

I was really impressed by my friend's haven in Utah. And a little jealous. Until I read the FBI's crime statistics. The murder rate in Utah was half that of New York . . . but higher than that of fourteen other states. And the rape, bur- glary and theft rates were substantially higher than New York's. (I used New York as my yardstick because everyone knows that *everything* happens in New York.)

It's probable that the unlocked door policy will never bring harm to my friend or his family, but as I listened to the pride of these people living in a neighborhood in which they felt confident in sleeping with their doors unlocked, what struck me was their naïveté. Criminals aren't likely to walk down the street trying doorknobs until they find one unlocked, although my friend told me that there was one in- cident in which someone with drug-fried brains was caught coming down the street trying doorknobs.

You don't lock your doors at night because there is a high risk that you will be murdered or raped during the night— you lock your doors because there is *some risk,* some small chance, and the "things" you are waging are not just your TV and stereo, but your life and that of your spouse and children.

With the stakes so high, why gamble with your family's lives?

And something else struck me about the arrangement: My friend has four children. What sort of security con- sciousness are these kids going to carry out of that house- hold when they enter the rough, cruel world? Unless they plan to spend their entire lives on that cozy street in Salt Lake City, these kids are not going to develop that aware- ness of the dangers in the environment around them. I have no doubt that these wonderful children will develop into fine young adults with great moral character, but I'm afraid that they won't know much about how to avoid personal harm to them and their families because they never learned that animals in the jungle don't sleep with their doors un-locked but find a tree or a cave to be secure in.

I heard much the same story about door locking when we visited friends in a small town in Montana. They are from the Big City and moved to a Sweet-Little-Montana-Town. They boasted to us that they not only do not lock their doors at night, but in warm weather, they commonly leave the front door open with just the screen door closed when they go to bed at night.

Wow. Another town in America on the verge of the New Millennium, where you don't need to lock the doors. It re-minded me of the Good Old Days. I was raised in small towns (nasty little places with railroad tracks), and when I was a kid we didn't lock the doors, not even after I woke up one night and found men with drawn guns in my bed-room . . . cops looking for my brother who had been in-volved in a fight. (It was a small town and the police took fighting serious, especially if you lived on the wrong side of the tracks.)

But funny thing . . . as I was getting out of our friend's car in front of their house after driving around the half dozen blocks that comprise the Sweet-Little-Montana-Town, I started to lock the car door and then stopped, com-menting to my friend that I guess he doesn't lock his car doors, either.

I was wrong—he *does* lock his car doors. He says kids in the neighborhood will steal anything you leave in the car.

Did I miss something here? They sleep with their front door *open* and their back door *unlocked* . . . but they lock their car doors to protect the sunglasses they leave on the seat?

More About House/ Apartment Alarm Systems

Let's talk a little more about security alarms, whether you're looking at a do-it-yourself system or contacting a security company.

An alarm system whether you buy and install it yourself, or hire a professional, basically consists of the same elements.

First, there are sensors that can be placed on doors and windows. There are various ways these sensors attach to the opening: They can be hard-wired by drilling from the attic or basement, connected by wire strung along baseboards, or radio-controlled without wiring.

When you set the alarm, a current flows through the sensors, letting the control box know that the door or window is secure. When the door or window is opened, the current flowing through the sensor is broken, and the alarm goes off.

The alarm is a horn that makes a hell of a lot of noise. It is usually mounted inside your house, but depending on local ordinances, you can have one outside that will alert the whole neighborhood (but with the number of false alarms we set off by forgetting the alarm is on, an outside horn is not always a great idea).

For homes and apartments with too many doors and windows to deal with economically in terms of a sensor for each, you can have motion detectors installed. Rather than operating when the door or window is opened, a motion detector goes off when someone enters the room (it puts out a pretty wide beam). Motion detectors can play hell with your life if you have a pet or small child who is going to set them off.

Motion detectors can often be set in a position where they cover more than one room at once. For example, some common physical layouts for apartments may permit one motion detector to cover an entire living room, dining room, and kitchen, literally a whole one-bedroom apartment since you wouldn't have a motion detector in a room where you sleep. You would then have the control panel in your bedroom and would turn off the system in the morning before you staggered out to the kitchen to fix coffee.

Besides the sensors (or motion detectors) that set off the horn, and the horn itself, there is the control panel mentioned above. Control panels are used to turn the system on and off (to "arm" and "disarm" the system). Many systems can be alarmed selectively or by zone—for example, during the evening you have the option to turn on the "perimeter" alarms (the ones connected to doors and windows) but not the motion detectors. That way your house is alarmed but you can still move around inside the house. When you go to bed you reset the alarm so that the perimeter and motion detectors are both working if not all the doors and windows are wired to the system.

Obviously, you do not have motion detectors in any room in which people will be sleeping, going down a hallway to a bathroom, or a pet will be running around (big families with lots of kids and pets may have to stick to door and window sensors rather than motion detectors).

The control panel is turned on and off by the use of a secret code, usually a three- or four-digit number (like your ATM code) that you program in. When you set the alarm, it takes thirty to forty-five seconds for the alarm to activate. The delay is to allow you to open an alarmed door and leave the house if you are going away. When you return, there is another thirty- to forty-five-second delay in the horn going off to allow you to get to the control panel and turn off the alarm.

Most systems have battery backup. That means that the system still operates in case of a power failure (or if someone turns off your power at the electric box outside most homes).

In most areas "monitoring" is also available. Monitoring is done via your telephone line. The alarm company sets up the system in your house or apartment and wires it so that when it goes off, a signal is sent over your phone line to their control station. The control stations are manned 24 hours a day. When the emergency signal is received, personnel at the control station will call you to ascertain whether you are all right. (Whether they call you will depend on the type of signal they receive—most alarm systems come with a panic button or a special code you tap into the control panel. If the signal is from the panic button or special code, usually the police are sent out immediately rather than a call to you from the alarm company.)

The reason the alarm company calls you when they receive an ordinary alarm signal is because there are so many false alarms—usually caused by people entering the house and forgetting to turn off the alarm in that thirty-to-forty-five-second grace period you get before it starts blasting away. Some of us, including myself, go traipsing out the rear patio doors on beautiful weekend mornings . . . and forget to turn off the alarm before we go out. It is a quicker "waker-upper" than a pot of coffee.

When the alarm company calls to find out if you need assistance, you either give them an "all-clear" code (a secret word that you reveal to no one except members of the household) or you give them the wrong response (for example, your secret all-clear code is "France" and you give them "Italy"). When the alarm company gets the wrong response they send the police out. The idea is that the person holding the gun to your head (assuming they are not long gone because of the ear-shattering horn that is going off all this time) will not know that you are not giving the right response.

There are also patrol services that might be available for your neighborhood. Whether you want to invest in a monthly fee for these services will depend upon where you live and what you can afford. If you can afford one (or can't afford to be without one), do sign up. Do they do any good? I don't know. The last time I called the police it took them forty-five minutes to respond. The patrol service was quicker.

I suppose there are people who have been murdered in their bed in homes equipped with the finest alarm systems . . . just as people sometimes die in accidents while wearing their seat belts. Anything is possible, but I will take my chance anytime in a house with an alarm system over one without it.

And because of new technology, you can afford a home-security system whether you own a big house or rent a one-room apartment. The do-it-yourself systems can be taken with you when you move, and many of the professional alarm companies offer the same benefit even when the systems are hard-wired.

To reemphasize a point that I make constantly: *I am big on protecting life, not property* (although my computer is like a member of the family to me). There's no question that alarms are great for protecting your property while you are away. But to tell you the truth, I personally have little concern about my property (except my computer!). The main reason I have an alarm system is to protect my life and those of my family (and my computer).

I wouldn't own a car without seat belts (even if the law

didn't require them). The danger of serious injury or death is so much greater without a seat belt that it would not make any sense to have a car without them.

In my mind, residential alarm systems fall under about the same reasoning. We spend many thousands of dollars maintaining a residence, whether it is a small apartment or big house, and an alarm system, whether it is do-it-yourself or professionally installed, adds very little to the overall cost of living.

We are in an age in which you should think as much about protecting yourself as pleasuring yourself, as much about your personal safety as your personal health.

16

Personal Safety on the Streets
Don't leave home without it!

Down these mean streets a man must go who is not himself mean, who is neither tarnished nor afraid.

—Raymond Chandler

We inadvertently create the opportunities for criminals to victimize us when we walk, jog, and bike at odd hours or places where we are out of sight of others even momentarily. We carry our lack of security consciousness into parking lots at the supermarket and the mall. Personal safety deserves as much consideration as what we eat and how we live. With a plague of crime on the streets, get security smart and street-smart by giving thought to your personal safety.

We can't stay home our whole life, barricaded behind locked doors, waiting for the bogeyman with an assault rifle in our sweaty palms. Nor can we go out in body armor (unless you're into robbing banks or a member of a SWAT team). But we can set up lines of resistance to crime, even random crime, by maintaining an awareness of our own vulnerability and that of our loved ones.

Personal safety, like security anywhere, depends much upon attitude. We either have or develop the right attitude or we go on being a victim from one type of situation to another in life and hope that we don't create an opportunity for a violent attack on ourselves or someone we love.

Maintaining the right attitude, that security consciousness, will help keep us out of the wrong place at the wrong time. And will keep us from making every place we go the wrong place.

If you don't believe that some people don't send out a scent that says "take advantage of me" like panicked swimmers do for sharks, you haven't met my friend Carol.

Carol is a lovely, intelligent, bright-eyed enthusiastic charmer; however she is not very observant when it comes to personal security. When my wife and I went to New York with Carol, her purse was stolen. When we went to England with Carol, her wallet was stolen. In Rome, when Gypsy children suddenly swarmed us on the street, they took her wallet and passport out of her purse. One Gypsy girl actually had her hand inside my coat before I realized what she was doing, but none of my valuables were stolen—my wallet was in a special inside zippered coat pocket, and my passport, most of my money and credit cards were in a concealed pouch strapped to my ankle (I know, *you* think *I* think I'm Mr. Perfect. I don't, and I'm not; it just happens that I had read guidebooks about Rome, took the warnings about Gypsies seriously, and brought a travel jacket with an inside zippered pocket).

It does no good to tell Carol to pay more attention when she's on the street—she is simply not security conscious.

The security problem with Carol is that she simply doesn't

maintain an awareness of what is going on around her. She is very animated and excited much of the time, and that makes her more attentive toward things that have caught her attention for the moment rather than the fact that the sky might be falling. By not paying attention to her surroundings, she turns almost anyplace into the wrong place.

Sometimes terrible things happen no matter how prepared we are. But they also happen *more frequently* to people who are not prepared because they are unconscious of the dangers around them. Remember those horror pictures taken from a helicopter of a man being dragged out of his truck and beaten half to death during the Los Angeles riots? Did someone open his truck door and drag him out? Would he have been dragged out of his truck if *his doors had been locked* as he drove through a section of the city that has been notorious for crime and racial strife?

What are the odds of someone locking the doors if they are driving a company car or truck? Probably not as common as when they're driving their own vehicle. If the driver who was beaten had been driving his own car, he might have had the doors locked if he was forced to go through a "bad" area. Why is it different when we're in a company vehicle? Because we get into a mental set driving a company vehicle, a frame of mind that we are somehow immune to the dangers on the street, that the situation is somehow different than being in our own vehicle, that perhaps we are even protected by the invisible shield of our employer.

Work is a place we go and for those hours of a day are in a cocoon, under the "protection" of our employer. We carry that mentality with us when we drive the company car.

Some personal safety habits should just be common sense: We have talked about using an ATM machine at night, and it is common sense that at night you never use one that is outside. That bit of common sense, if used by everyone, would save hundreds of lives every year, but people insist upon taking the risk. If you desperately have to use an ATM card at night, play the *Dollars vs. Life* game and realize that you are betting a dollar or two against your life. Many people who throw away money on lotteries that are millions-to-one long shots aren't willing to pay a couple of dollars to avoid even shorter odds that they might get murdered using an outside ATM machine at night.

A man was shot to death at an ATM machine near the same intersection as the truck incident . . . murdered as he stopped to use the machine at *three o'clock in the morning.* What sort of mental set was he in? He worked nights and had stopped by and used the machine dozens of times in the middle of the night—maybe *hundreds* of times. What he didn't take into consideration was the law of averages. If you keep playing Russian roulette, the odds are that you will ultimately pay for it. Getting away with a dangerous activity hundreds of times only means that the odds are building up against you.

Remember the tragic story of the businesswoman attacked by a whole gang of young creeps while jogging in Central Park . . . a well-used jogging path, but one that occasionally put her out of sight of other joggers and was next to a high-crime area. (Is there anywhere that isn't near a high-crime area anymore???) Had she taken that same run hundreds of times? Was there a safer place she could have run, a place that perhaps was not as pleasant or as convenient, but where the odds of avoiding harm were better?

Are these unusual cases? Not at all. People are consistently getting assaulted because they fail to lock their car doors, they use ATM machines at the wrong time, and because they jog in places where they pass out of sight, even momentarily, of other joggers.

Bad things can happen to anyone at any time, and I only point these incidents out because they made headlines. And because the particular incidents, as tragic as they were for the victims, provide lessons that might save others.

The next several sections point out things that should become second nature to you and your family, *safety* habits just as putting on your seat belt after getting into your car and looking both ways before crossing a street have been ingrained in you.

The recommendations center around the premise of personal security: becoming security conscious so that regardless of where you are, or what you are doing, you lessen your chance of becoming a victim.

When you leave your house to shop, walk, jog, bike, go out to dinner, see a movie, or visit friends, besides your keys and wallet take along a security awareness that can protect your life.

Don't create trouble for yourself by failing to use a little common sense and a few precautions.

Jogging, Walking, Biking

The tale of a young businesswoman attacked by a gang of crazies is a tragic story. The woman was on a popular jogging path when attacked, but it was a path that frequently took a jogger *out of sight* of other joggers. This is especially dangerous if you plan to jog during odd hours. "Out of sight" is the wrong place to jog. When you add "odd hours" it becomes an even more dangerous formula because it creates an opportunity for criminals that they would not otherwise have.

There are random and capricious elements to crime. There are situations where you will be in the wrong place and wrong time no matter what you do. But let's take a closer look at jogging and walking.

Why is a person jogging or walking chosen to be the victim of a crime? If you are a woman, and the crime has a sexual motive, that certainly would be a factor. And if you're in the same general area as a criminal looking for an opportunity to prey on someone, it's another factor. But the key word here is "opportunity." Being a woman and jogging in and of itself does not create the opportunity. A person will be chosen for a crime because they are jogging where a criminal has come to commit a crime, and has provided the opportunity for the criminal by getting exercise at an inappropriate place and/or time.

We can't stop being who we are, and getting exercise is good for us, but we have to give some thought about safety because criminals are everywhere in our society. We no longer have a country in which you can simply walk out of your residence or take a jog at any time of the day or night and not have personal safety concerns. When you do these things at odd hours it increases the danger.

What are *odd hours?*

Times when other people are usually not around. There is a certain amount of safety in numbers, not because the people will necessarily come to your rescue, but because they can sound the alarm that will bring police.

Don't jog, ride your bike, or take nature walks at *odd* hours when other people are not engaged in the same activity. I don't care how often you have done it, how many years you have lived in the neighborhood and walked that same path. You are just increasing your odds of finding trouble.

People who exercise by walking, jogging, and bike riding can get themselves into another type of mental set. Why are these people exercising? For their health. Why won't they put greasy food into their stomachs that over a period of many years can give them cancer? For their health. Then why do so many of these *healthy* types get mugged every year because they are off the beaten path or out at odd hours? Because they are more concerned about their health than their lives. . . .

The evening I wrote the above statement, my wife and I were returning from a movie, and my wife pointed out a young woman jogging on the dark street in a residential neighborhood. She was wearing short shorts and a halter top. She wasn't wearing a jogging bra, and her breasts bounced with every step. My wife said she was a human sign saying—*Attack me!*

If we had stopped and talked to the woman we may have found out that she has been making the same run down the dark street hundreds of times and never had a problem. Okay, I can buy that. The guy using the ATM machine late at night never had a problem before, either . . . until he *had* that one problem that took his life.

Neither the jogger nor the ATM user gave any thought to what they were risking.

You can leave your bike unchained outside the coffee bar when you go in for your cappuccino hundreds of times. One day your bike is gone. You risked your bike, and now you have to buy a new one.

But risking your *life* is different.

Does a person jogging anywhere, anytime, have a risk of getting harmed?

There is some risk, yes.

If the person is a woman, does the risk go up?

Unfortunately, yes.

If the woman is jogging alone at night down a dark street, does the risk go up even further?

Yes.

And what is she risking? Her wristwatch? A couple of bucks in a belly pack? Or her life?

There is a difference between solitude and increasing risk. Unfortunately, women are much more at risk with the type of nut who would bother a jogger or bike rider than a man. Anything can happen to anyone anywhere, but there are greater chances of something happening if you fit certain criteria or provide the opportunity. Again, some things, like where we live and our sex, we can't do anything about, but we can be aware of the increased danger and take steps to lessen it.

Think about the risk factors before you blindly do things:

- A woman would likely be a victim while jogging, etc., because of the possibility of a sexual motive that is usually not present in an attack of a man.
- Anyone who jogs, bikes, etc. at places less frequented by others increases the risks, whether they are a man or woman.
- Jogging, biking, etc. at odd hours—after dark or when others are not around.
- Being out-of-sight of others on lonely stretches (this isn't as bad with bikes as it is with jogging or taking walks because bikes move so much faster).
- Living in an urban area as opposed to a rural area (the closer to the heart of the city, or large pockets of lower-income housing, the greater the danger—but suburban areas which have fewer people around can also increase the danger because there is some strength in numbers).
- Not carrying and having readily available a personal alarm.

A personal alarm that fits on your key chain, your belly pack, or on a clip attached to a clothing loop is a "panic button" that you should not be without while walking, jogging, going to the store at night, taking an evening class at the local college, or any other activity that puts you at extra risk, especially if you are a woman. (As noted above, being female is a risk factor in and of itself for many activities—have you ever heard of a man being dragged into the bushes and raped walking to his car from a night class?)

Everyone I know who has had one of these personal alarms ends up putting it in a dresser drawer because the person never uses them. These people who toss a security device aside because they aren't getting attacked are missing the point. The point is not that you are going to use it every day or even once in a while. The reason you have it is to have a security device that *one time in your life* when you need it.

The second problem is that people who have purchased them don't keep them handy enough. Having the alarm in your pocket or your purse is not going to help when someone is dragging you into the bushes.

You can pick these personal alarms up at a discount store for a few dollars or invest much more in a higher quality, compact model that is much less bulky than the cheaper variety.

Here again, the device should be kept handy or it won't be any use at all. Joggers, bike riders, and walkers commonly clip the personal panic button to their clothes.

But also be aware that there is a danger with the keyless entries and personal alarms: *overconfidence.* Don't think you can go walking, jogging or bike riding in places where you shouldn't just because you have a noisemaker. The personal alarm isn't going to help unless you are in an area where other people are so close they will be instantly alerted to your problem. And that assumes that people who heard it will come to your rescue.

The second danger is using a personal alarm at the wrong time. When someone has a gun on you, give them what they want—making an annoying noise with a personal alarm would not be politically correct or socially perceptive.

And don't forget that each of us has a built-in alarm system as good as any personal alarm: a pair of lungs that can let out a good scream or shouts for help.

Reacting to Street Violence

There are several possible scenarios to potential street violence, and we have to match our reaction correctly to the situation.

If somebody wants our property—our car, purse, wallet—we should give it to them instantly and run like hell, making as much noise as we can—unless they have a gun. If they have a gun, we should give them whatever they want and remain calm and passive. Property can be replaced, but we have only one life to lose.

You never argue or make noise when confronted with a person with a gun. You usually don't even try to reason with a stranger with a gun—you just try to remain calm and give them what they want.

I was once crossing a busy street in a bad neighborhood at night when a nut shoved a .45 automatic in my stomach. I remained calm and stood talking to him in a low voice for what seemed like an eternity (but was probably no more than a couple of minutes). It was a busy street, and people were lying down on the sidewalks. A motorcycle cop suddenly arrived—I don't know if he was called or just happened on the scene. He crouched down behind his bike with his gun drawn and yelled at the man. I stood perfectly still as the officer and the man shouted at each other. A moment later another motorcycle officer came up in the opposite direction. He got off his motorcycle and as the one officer kept up a dialogue with the man the other officer crept up behind the man and whacked the guy in the back of the head with his nightstick.

The courage of the two officers was incredible. And the way they handled the situation probably saved my life, the nut's life, and that of bystanders.

This incident happened some years ago, and I wonder how the situation would be handled today. In this age of street shoot-outs, in which criminals kill indiscriminately and police officers shoot back, I often wonder if the police officers would not have simply shot the man with me caught in the cross fire. I also wonder today if the man with the gun could have been kept talking first by me and then by the officer—or would he have simply started shooting because today that seems to be the way nuts do things.

I also deserve credit for remaining calm and speaking to the man in a low tone, asking him why he wanted to kill me, one question leading to another, always keeping my tone low and my eyes locked with his. I managed to unconsciously keep him occupied in a dialogue with me that kept him from concentrating on shooting me. The guy was drunk and drugged up, and I imagine a drunk or nut can be like a small child that can't chew gum and walk at the same time—as long as his mind was occupied answering questions about his motivations, he didn't pull the trigger.

While I give myself credit for remaining calm and talking to the man, the fact that I survived was also a matter of the luck of the draw: I was confronted by a crazy who did not simply go berserk and start shooting. With berserkers, you just hit the ground and play dead . . . if you aren't already dead.

In the incident with the gun on me, the bystanders were

smart—they got down, lying in the street until the police had the situation under control.

The incident with the gun on me took place in a bad neighborhood in a big city. But the only neighbors I knew that were murdered by thieves were not killed in bad neighborhoods, but in their own upscale residential neighborhoods because crime has become mobile.

One murder happened to my neighbor across the street a few years ago.

We lived in a nice neighborhood, but crime has become mobile, especially in urban areas. Late one evening my neighbor was escorting guests to their car parked in front of his house when a van pulled up and a shotgun poked out the window. The gunman demanded their wallets. No one knows why my neighbor reacted as he did, but instead of just standing there, he spun around to step back to the house. The shotgun went off and my neighbor was killed instantly. A friend suspected that the neighbor, a very nice young man who tended to be a bit hyper, might have spun around to go into the house to get his wallet for the robbers. Whatever the reason, the *sudden movement* cost him his life.

Don't make sudden movements when someone has a gun on you. Obviously, if someone starts shooting, you should get down, but if someone has a gun on you and simply wants something, like your wallet, don't make any sudden moves.

When a man with a gun stepped out from the bushes as another neighbor of mine was taking a walk, the man handed over his wallet. His wife put their lives into even worse jeopardy by turning and running. While she may have had good instincts in terms of running from trouble, it's a little hard to outrun a bullet.

Another friend parked at a McDonald's to let his son run inside. As he waited, a man stepped up to his car (a Mercedes) and pointed a gun at his head. The robber demanded his wallet and when my friend passed it over, the robber was disgusted because there was only $22 in it and said he should kill him. My friend kept very calm and lamented that he did not have more money to give the robber. At that point my friend's son, a young man in his twenties, came out of the restaurant. He gave the robber his money (he has less than $5) and explained in a very low and calm voice that he was sorry, that was all the money they had, but he was sure if the man kept trying he would find someone with more money.

The idea of moving on to fresh game seemed to appeal to the robber because he left.

There is no question that my friend and his son handled the matter exactly right by staying calm and speaking in a low voice. There is also no question that they were amazingly lucky even though they did exactly the right things. The way I look at it, at the moment the gun was pointed at them, there was a thin line between living and dying, and they managed to straddle that line with their actions.

In almost any circumstance other than someone with a gun, my opinion is that you should run like hell and make as much noise as possible. I would do this even if it was someone with a knife unless the person had the knife against my body or close enough to strike.

I am not suggesting that I'd struggle over money—if a person with a knife wants my wallet, I'll leave it behind before I run. But I'm not going to let myself be led anywhere by a knife wielder unless the knife is against my body.

When I suggest being passive in the face of loss of property, I don't stretch that to being passive when someone wants to harm me or my loved ones. And while the best defense is a fast pair of feet and a lot of noise in most cases, when I'm a trapped rat I would lash out and fight back.

Going Out to Eat, Movies, Shopping

Eating Out

There's a restaurant I like to go to when I don't feel like really going out, a nice cozy place where you just drop in for a quick meal—good pasta and wine at a price that lets you pretend it would cost as much to eat at home. It has a large parking lot in back, well lit, but there's no security guard, no back entrance to the restaurant, no back windows, and the lot feels a little isolated. The restaurant is in a decent business area, but a few blocks from a low-income "high-crime" area. The restaurant faces a busy street, and because the restaurant itself is busy, there usually isn't parking in front and if you want to park on the street you may have to walk a block.

Where do I park when I go there to eat? Not in the well-lighted parking lot—I take my chance on the busy street out front and walk the extra block.

Before you read below, can you pick out the reasons I avoid the parking lot?

These are my reasons:

- There is no guard or valet parking attendant in the parking lot.
- People inside the restaurant cannot see the parking lot.
- The parking lot cannot be seen from the main street.
- A "bad area" begins a few blocks away.
- There's a busy street out front I can park on.
- The extra block I walk helps get rid of some pasta calories.

I would take a *busy* street over an isolated parking lot anytime. Bad things happen on busy streets but they happen *less frequently* than in parking lots.

I would take outdoor parking over *unsecured* indoor parking most of the time.

Indoor parking, covered or underground, takes you out of the public view and sometimes increases your chance of getting mugged or worse. I prefer secured lots where there is a guard or attendant around.

Valet parking is the best of all worlds if there is any threat that you will be some crazy bastard's after-dinner dessert.

I am not paranoid that I will be mugged or raped in a parking lot when I go out to dinner—I wouldn't go to a restaurant or anywhere else if I had to worry about danger.

I just instinctively maintain a sense of awareness about where I park, the same as I do about putting on my seat belt or looking both ways before I cross the street. If I don't like the looks of a situation, I will move away from it.

We all make those kind of choices, and we don't really think about it—you probably don't eat at the favorite haunts of gangbangers and drug dealers. Not because you're paranoid, but because you're not stupid.

I just carry it a little further—I consider it stupid to park in an isolated parking lot at night and take even a very small risk of harm when I can park on a busy street and take a much lesser risk of harm.

The thought process isn't much different than that of choosing a financial institution with an FDIC guarantee for your money over one without a guarantee. What I find strange is that so many people give more thought to their *financial security* than their *personal security*. The chances of losing your money due to a bank failure are extremely low. But many of the same people who would not think of putting their money in a bank without an FDIC guarantee won't invest a few hundred dollars in a home alarm system that might protect their family. . . .

I make this point repeatedly because it is something that people have to overcome. They have to realize that their personal security is entitled to as much concern as their health and financial welfare.

When you leave the house, give as much thought about where you put your body as you do where you have placed your money.

Movies

I have one piece of advice for going to movies: *Keep your mouth shut.*

I never talk in movies (one of the greatest sins I can imagine) but I have unfortunately opened my mouth a few times to people who insisted upon talking. This was in the days when my bones did not break as easily as they do now and in days in which the worst that could happen to me was to have someone pop me in the mouth. Today, you can get killed.

I learned my lesson when I was on vacation with my wife in Pacific Grove, California, a sweet, classy seaside village famous for its scenic beauty and the butterflies that flock there every year. This is a very nice little town, bordered by the Pacific Ocean, scenic Monterey, rich old Carmel, and the haute Pebble Beach Country Club thrown somewhere in between.

While we were watching the movie a young man and two young women behind us started gabbing away. I turned around and asked the young man to please be quiet. They shut up, but I immediately heard one of the young women whisper, "We should kill him."

This incident happened within the last couple of years,

and you can tell from reading this book how security conscious I am. So you know that I would have grabbed my wife and rushed out into the lobby, yelling for the popcorn attendant to call the police.

Well, I didn't exactly do that. What I did was . . . nothing. It just didn't bother me. When I had turned to say something to the young man I had sized him up: he was a little chunky, in his early twenties, and dressed in regular (i.e., not gangbanger) clothing. There was nothing threatening in his demeanor. When I politely asked him to be quiet, he was polite and looked concerned. In other words, a pretty average, ordinary guy. They had shut up after my request (other than the woman's comment). So we sat there, watched the movie, munched popcorn and thought nothing about the incident. (Actually, my wife had not heard the girl's whispered comment.)

We were leaving the theater at an ordinary pace when I noticed the young man hurrying away, and I thought to myself, gee, I must be a tougher-looking dude than I thought (I'm not tough-looking at all). Then I saw him looking back at two young women and realized they must be the girls he had been sitting with. I had not gotten a look at either woman in the theater, had only seen them from the back as they left in front of us, and now as I got a good look at them I didn't feel so brave. These were a couple of mean-looking street-trash, gangbangers; one of them had a dripping dagger tattoo under her eye. These two glared at me, challenging me with their looks to step away from the crowd coming out of the theater.

I thought, oh shit, now I've done it. I grabbed my wife and pulled her into a restaurant. We left the restaurant in a taxi and I paid the driver extra to take us all of three blocks to our hotel.

What bothers me most about the incident is that I opened

my mouth and put someone else into danger (my wife). What also bothers me is that I didn't get my wife out when I heard the threat. I can't explain why I wasn't bothered when I heard the girl whisper about killing me in the theater. I think it was a combination of things—being on vacation, being in a sweet little town, having sized up the young man and not believing he was trouble, and *not* having gotten a look at what a couple of really hard women I was offending.

And maybe it was a "man thing"—up to that time I hadn't given much thought as to how physically dangerous a woman can be. The stories in the media about teenage girls being initiated into gangs by having to kill someone didn't come home until I saw those two young women. The last time I had seen the dripping dagger tear on anyone was on a 220-pound gangbanger fresh out of prison, and I had defended him for beating someone half to death on his way back to prison.

I think also that my love for movies and theaters lulled me into feeling safe. Movie houses are sanctuaries to me, and I don't expect trouble in them any more than I would at church.

Theaters are usually very safe places, but we get a mixed bag of people in them, and you never know who you are going to take on when you tell someone to shut up so you can enjoy the movie. I got into a shouting match with a woman in a theater when she permitted her three-year-old to continuously kick the back of my seat. When I asked her politely to have the kid stop, she told me that he was only three years old. I made the mistake of pointing out that she wasn't three . . . and she went ballistic.

In another theater I told three young college-age men to shut up and the only thing that kept me from getting my head ripped off was the fact other people joined in a chorus for them to shut up.

My new rules for dealing with idiots in movies is to keep my mouth shut and wait for someone with more courage than I to tell them to shut up. Lacking anyone standing up for my right to quiet enjoyment of the movie, I change seats.

I don't even bother to get an usher. First, I don't believe ushers are able to handle the type of nuts we get in theaters anyway, not to mention a recent killing in a theater after an irate patron came back with an usher to confront a noise-maker, and the noisemaker pulled out a gun and blew away the patron. There was a time when a uniformed usher would have symbolized authority to a movie patron, but the world was just a bit different in those days.

Shopping

When shopping most people park as close as they can to the store and sometimes that is a long ways from the nearest entrance. They have done it a thousand times and the reflex is automatic—they go there, they park, they walk in thinking about their purchases.

Why is it that so many people, especially women, will become victims of crime in a mall parking lot? Is it where they park? That could be one factor, but where you park may be the thing you have the least control over.

The fact that the person is alone is certainly another factor.

But there is a third factor that plays as much of a role as the other two. That is attitude. Too many of us simply are not security conscious when we go to the mall. We park our car or walk back to our car without giving the slightest thought about who or what is around us or what we would do if we are attacked. When trouble comes, we are so surprised and stunned that we are unable to react.

We also don't think about the fact that a good percentage of us have a personal security device available. If we have a car alarm, there is usually a panic button on the remote we carry. Most people are not even aware that most car alarms include this panic-button feature. And even fewer people keep their alarm remote in hand and ready to use, so having the equipment does nothing for them anyway.

If you have a car-alarm panic button or a personal security device, keep it ready. It's true few of us get excited anymore about car alarms—but mall security still does, and, if nothing else, people automatically look in that direction when they hear an alarm go off.

We don't have to fear going to the mall. But somewhere between being fearful and being totally blind to any potential danger is simply being expedient.

When we walk to and from our car, we need to keep our eyes open and maintain an awareness of our surroundings.

We should have our keys in hand for faster entry into our car even if we are carrying packages. Standing by our car to rummage into our purse or pocket for our keys is a vulnerable moment because we will be focusing on that chore.

Lock your car door when you are getting in instead of waiting to lock it after you are settled. While you are getting settled into the driver's seat is another time when you are very vulnerable to criminal attack.

And have a talk with yourself about what you do when trouble hits. You have much less chance of becoming a victim if you have a personal safety attitude and have given at least a little thought to how you would handle an attack. A good pair of lungs to scream with and a swift pair of feet are usually the best defense against any crime.

There are other commonsense attitudes you should develop about shopping.

Don't shop at night when you can avoid it because most rapes, robberies and other violent crimes occur at night. If you work all day and you can only shop at night, be aware that your chances of being a victim have risen.

Avoid going into liquor stores and minimarts at night. These places are high on the list of criminals both in terms of attacking patrons coming in or out and robbing the premises. Do without that urgent quart of milk when you are on your way home from a movie or go to a larger store with good lighting and maybe even a security guard.

Prohibitions about leaving small children outside in cars while you go inside stores to shop are too obvious to take the time to deal with. Just don't do it, period.

If you stop at a supermarket or minimart and pop inside, leaving your spouse or older children in the car, take your keys with you and make sure the doors are locked. Taking your keys makes it harder for someone to jump into the car and drive off with your family.

If you have the choice between the discount market where there is no guard in the lot and a high-price market where there is a security guard, think about the *Dollars vs. Life* factor.

When you are pushing the shopping cart to your car keep your eyes open and your keys in hand.

Don't be paranoid but maintain an awareness of your surroundings. Take the same precautions whether it is daytime or nighttime but maintain a higher degree of awareness at night.

Don't expect anyone else to be responsible for your security. If there was anyone around to help, you probably wouldn't be attacked in the first place.

Personal Safety Checklist

1. Maintain an awareness of your surroundings, no matter where you go. Don't walk from the mall to your car at night without keeping your eyes open. You can think about anything you like, just maintain a habit of being more security conscious when it is nighttime and you are alone, or you are jogging or biking out of sight of others.
2. Own a personal security device and keep it handy. If you walk to your car at night, from a movie, the mall, dinner, night school, keep the personal security device handy.
3. Follow your instincts—if a situation bothers you, don't step into it. Have the guts to walk away. Or run away.
4. Don't jog, take walks, or bike at odd hours.
5. Take secured parking anytime you are out at night. Pay the extra pennies to shop at a secured supermarket. Pay the extra money for valet parking.
6. If you have a choice between street parking and isolated parking, take the street parking.
7. Keep your mouth shut in theaters. If there are rude idiots around you who won't keep their mouth shut, move to another area of the theater. If that means they win, hey, that's okay—*you* never win when you take on a crazy.
8. If you are one of those fight-it-to-death types and insist upon going out and reporting the noisy theater patron to the management, ask

them to give you time to return to a seat (on the other side of the theater, if you have any sense) before they confront the noisemakers. That way the troublemakers hopefully won't identify you as the stool pigeon.

9. Don't get onto an elevator alone if there is someone on it that sends your paranoia soaring. Don't be a wimp—if you don't like the situation, step out before you are trapped inside. If you are in a relatively deserted area, don't stand close to the elevator doors when they are opening. At Los Angeles International Airport, one of the busiest airports in the world, several women were assaulted when a man pulled them into the elevator when the doors opened, and he saw them standing alone.

10. If you are confronted with a gun, don't argue. Give them everything but your life.

11. Your best defense is almost always a swift pair of feet and healthy lungs—running and screaming is the preferred defense to almost any situation—other than someone with a gun on you.

12. If you are a woman, don't let Macho Jack, your cool dude boyfriend, get you into situations that endanger you. You will end up as pet food after some animal eats Jack alive.

13. If you are a man, don't let Macho Betty get you into danger. Tell her not to pick fights with any dudes she can't handle herself. (The age of chivalry was killed by women's rights. I once made an ass out of myself on a Caribbean cruise during an abandon-ship drill

by loudly insisting that the women-and-children-first tradition went out with Affirmative Action. Those were the days when I still stood up for my rights and argued over every injustice. I was just kidding, of course. I want women to go first . . . my shipboard emergency kit is a wig and a dress.)

14. Don't use an ATM machine after dark or during odd hours when others aren't around. Don't risk your life to save a couple of bucks. ATMs are popping up in more and more well-lit, safe stores and malls. When you desperately need the money, pay the extra fee to use one of those.

15. Don't be overconfident. Don't park, drive, ride, sit, walk, jog or visit anyplace where you have the slightest doubt it isn't perfectly safe.

16. Maintain a steady sense of confidence even when things go to hell. Sometimes criminals pick out easy targets who they think won't fight back. Even if you won't fight back, don't leave that impression.

17. Try to avoid shopping at night. Avoid liquor stores and minimalls since these are high on the list for crime attacks.

18. Stay calm. Move fast when you need to. Freeze or hit the ground when you need to. But blind panic or erratic movements (like my neighbor who spun around with a shotgun pointed at him) can get you killed.

17

Road Rage and Breakdowns
Crazies on the road and in parking lots

According to the AAA Foundation for Traffic Safety, there have been over 10,000 incidents of road rage over a seven-year period. And the incidents have been rising 7% a year.

Forget the notion that your two-thousand-pound car provides any protection. There are guns in one-third of the cars in America, so the nut behind the wheel is liable to be armed and dangerous. This is not a big-city phenomenon—some parts of rural America have higher incidents of deadly road rage than the great metropolitan areas. Recognize your vulnerability while in a car. And if you are not going to take responsibility for your own safety by having a contingency plan and basic knowledge of the most common car breakdown problems, take a bus and leave the driving to them.

When I was in Britain a few years ago I saw a cartoon in a newspaper that showed people in two cars shooting at each other while on an American freeway. A third car was coming up between them, and someone in the third car says, "Don't worry, they're too drunk to hit anything." The caption on the cartoon was "Los Angeles Freeway."

Drunk and crazy is an apt description not just for metro freeways but roads all over America at night. In the first chapter of this book I related the story of Jenny and Jack and the crazy who turned Jenny's life into a lifetime nightmare. That incident didn't occur because Jenny lived in a big city—the state of Washington, which has more rivers and trees than people, has a greater incidence of violent road rage than most of the largest metro areas of the nation.

Cars used to provide more security—all that metal, that speed—between us and *them*. But with the increasing frequency of violence on our roadways and in our parking lots, if you're not security conscious, you're probably going to be roadkill.

If there is anywhere that false courage and machismo will raise their ugly heads, it's on the street in cars. All that metal and speed brings the courage out of guys who get sand kicked in their face at the beach and the fury out of women who run from mice.

Flipping the bird, shouting insults and obscenities, are par for the course to these road warriors.

In line at the post office, I heard a blue-hair, grandmotherly woman telling someone how she finally stands up for her rights and uses her horn to let stupid people on the road know they're idiots. The conversation stuck with me because on the way to the post office I had heard a radio news story about a *grandfather* shot in front of his two grandchildren when he honked his horn at some teenagers blocking his path in an alley. One of the teenagers simply pulled out a gun, walked up to the car, and shot him dead in front of the grandkids.

You hear about these road-rage idiots all the time, people taking out their stress and getting it off honking their horns, yelling obscenities at someone who cut them off in traffic—or even got close to cutting them off. And it's incredibly stupid and dangerous in a society in which a wrong turn can take you into gang territory or the middle of a drug deal. Not to mention the increasing number of ordinary crazies with guns on the road, just looking for someone to blow away.

If you're twenty years old, street violence may be just par for the course, life imitating movies, but some of us over forty can remember when expressions like "road rage" and drive-by shooting" weren't in our vocabulary, and we didn't lock our car doors.

Locked car doors serve not just a security function, but a safety one—passengers being ejected because car doors fly open in crashes is a major cause of traffic deaths. Automatic door locks are becoming a common feature in many new automobiles. However, the doors don't lock until a few seconds *after* the key is turned on. That may work nicely in regard to keeping you from being ejected in an accident, but as mentioned before, don't rely upon automatic door locks (if your car has them) for personal safety because if someone is going to jump into your car it will happen about the same time as you're off-balance in the process of entering.

When you purchase a car, buy the remote locking/unlocking and automatic door-lock features if it is an option. It will cost a little more, but the remote entry devices have good security features. Remote entry for your car is a good investment in the *Dollars vs. Life* calculation.

Remote entry devices usually have a *panic*-button feature. We already discussed the fact that you should get into the habit of carrying your car keys in your hand with the remote ready, especially when you are approaching your car in the dark, in bad areas, and underground parking lots where there is no attendant in sight. It's a good security-conscious habit because if someone is going to attack you, they are not going to wait until you dig in your pocket or your purse to get out your remote to hit the panic button.

A friend of mine tells me that when she works late and approaches her car in the dark parking lot at night she carries her keys so one key sticks out of her fist. Her plan is to poke an attacker in the eye. Not a bad idea . . . but my suggestion to her was: (1) If she knows she is going to work late, take a quick break and move the car as close as possible to the building exit while it's still daylight; (2) when she leaves at night, ask the door guard to keep an eye out for her; (3) hold her car's remote entry so that if someone comes near, she can instantly press the panic button on it.

She can still carry a key to stab someone in the eye, but in order of preference I would prefer to see her run and scream like hell and push the panic button to make more noise before she uses a car key to take on a two-hundred-pound psycho.

The other use for the keyless entry is that you can unlock and enter your car much faster than someone who has to fumble with keys in the dark while the bogeyman is sneaking up from behind.

Form Habits, Not Paranoia

Life isn't worth living if we have to worry about carjackers and maniacs every time we go shopping at night or work late and have to walk out to that dark and lonely parking lot.

So don't worry—the idea is not to worry about it, not even to think about it, but to form *habits* that will protect our life if an ugly situation arises. If we get in the habit of carrying our keys while walking to our car with the remote in hand and locking our doors immediately while stepping into our car, we will be ready to react. And we will be protecting the lives of our family members if we help them form the same good habits.

We should not resist a carjacker or do anything in any manner to keep one from taking our car. If they want our car, we should give it to them immediately without blinking an eye.

More About Cars

Night Driving

Driving at night takes a little more care in regard to security than daytime driving if for no other reason than more crimes are committed at night and on weekends than Monday through Friday during the day.

When you get gas at a self-service station, get in a habit of trying for a pump as close to the cashier booth as possible even if you are paying by credit card at the pump. The cashier isn't going to protect you from anyone, but there is less of a chance to become the victim of a crime when there is a witness and telephone handy.

You don't want to be a smart-ass in traffic anytime, but your chances of getting a bullet in the head for honking at the wrong person dramatically goes up at night when the creeps have come out under the cover of darkness.

Keep your doors locked, day or night.

Many supermarkets and general-merchandise "drug" stores in larger cities stay open twenty-four hours, but it is not advisable to do your shopping after nine o'clock at night even if it's not as busy. Fewer people coming and going in the parking lot drives up your chance of being the victim of a crime.

There have been a number of incidents in which a car gets "bumped" at night by another car, and the bumped driver dutifully pulls over to check the damage and exchange identification only to find that it was a setup to get them to stop. Women driving at night have especially been the victims of this scam.

If you have any doubt at all that the bump you get from another car is not a legitimate accident, do not pull over. Instead, signal the other driver to follow you and drive directly to a well-lighted, well-populated area to discuss the matter. If you have a cellular phone, use it to contact 911 and to tell them your fears.

You should understand that there is a thin line between wrongfully leaving the scene of an accident and enforcing your right to be secure. If you let the other driver know, without getting out of your car, of your intent, there should not be a problem. If I had to choose between an irked driver and my personal safety, my safety wins every time.

One of my clients involved in such an incident used driving away out of fear as an excuse after she left the scene of an accident because she had no insurance. Her story was a little weak because the police noted that she had driven miles home instead of to the nearest secure area and had not bothered reporting the matter to the police.

What should you do if the other person won't follow you? If you have advised them to follow you, and they choose not to, and you don't have a cellular phone to report the matter, I would report the matter as soon as I reached a phone by calling the police and giving them information about the accident.

Again, don't be inhibited. Don't be intimidated into getting out of your car in a place where you might be in danger. Obeying the law does not mean you have to jeopardize your life. Acting reasonably under the circumstances may mean you don't step out of your car on a lonely road because someone has caused a minor accident.

Be sure and call the police *before* the other person does.

By the way, in regard to security concerns in a car, if you are one of those people like me who bought a protective spray like pepper spray or mace when it became legal in your area, check your glove box to find out where it's at— by the time I get through rummaging in the box to find it to be able to use it, I would be a dead duck. I still recommend buying protective sprays (and stun guns and the like where legal), but I have to admit that remembering they are there and having them handy to use in an emergency may be a real long shot.

I believe you should have legal sprays and other protective devices in your vehicle, but those are mainly going to come in handy if you break down. They are not going to help if someone grabs you just as you are getting into your car.

Most of us are better able to use our wits to get out of tricky situations than using protective devices that we have to hunt to find. I have made the point that you cannot rely upon others to get you out of jams. Don't think you can rely on devices, either. Don't go places you wouldn't normally go just because you have a personal security device on your key chain or a protective spray in your purse or pocket. Some Neanderthal is liable to rip your head off before you can press the right button. If you have them, fine, have them available for use. But your best defense to any situation is not getting into the problem in the first place.

People Who Can't Change Flats Might End Up as Roadkill

In regard to personal safety, every person in the household with a driver's license should be taught certain fundamentals about automobiles, the least of which is how to change a flat tire. It would be pretty stupid to be out on a dark and lonely road and have a flat tire and not know how to use a spare and jack. If you don't think it can happen, note that the senseless, tragic death of Ennis Cosby came as a result of a flat tire on a busy Los Angeles freeway.

Emergency Equipment to Carry

What sort of emergency equipment should you carry in your car? I suggest the following:

1. Flashlight. I carry two: an eighteen-inch policeman-type flashlight that holds lots of batteries and can be used as a club in case of emergency, and one of those multipurpose lights that can emit a yellow flash to warn off oncoming cars in case of breakdown. I carry the policeman's flashlight within arm's reach of the driver's seat.
2. Fire extinguisher. One of those that are no more than six or seven inches high. They don't put out big fires, but I have used them to stop my own car fire and a fire in another car. By the way—car fires can be dangerous. I would not get near a car engulfed in flames—the fires I put out were in the engine compartment and

had just ignited. If you're wearing a coat and the fire is in the engine compartment, you can sometimes smother the flames with the coat.

I once ran up to a burning car with an extinguisher in hand, and the owner waved me away. "Let it burn," he said. "It's insured, and this way I get a new one." The car was already engulfed in flames, and I probably would have managed to get myself torched, anyway. Stay away from fires in motor homes. Motor homes usually carry propane besides gasoline.

3. Flares. Carry several. These are a real necessity. Also, don't try to figure out how to ignite a flare after you break down in the middle of the night and in heavy traffic. Study the instructions on the flare package when you buy it so you are at least familiar with the concept of how a flare is ignited.

4. Swiss Army knife. I can't count the times that one of these gems has come in handy, from slicing bread and cheese and opening a wine bottle on a picnic along the Rhine, to cutting gray adhesive tape when I wrapped a broken coolant hose. I carry one in the glove compartment of my car—*don't leave home without one.*

5. Legal protective devices. This will depend upon the laws of where you live: Typical items are pepper spray, mace, stun guns. To find out what you can carry in your car and if you need a license, check with your local gun and/or sporting-goods store because this is where these items are usually sold.

6. Cellular phone. This ranks only slightly under an assault rifle as a protective device. The problem is that they don't work everywhere (and never where you break down), but the range is getting better.

7. Spare coolant hoses, fan belts, and timing belt. You should carry these even if you are incapable of putting them on. You don't even have to buy spares: Tell your mechanic next time hoses are replaced for preventive maintenance, to give you the old ones. The reason to carry them is that your car will *always* break down at night and in places where the gas station you get towed to *never* has the right size hoses and belts. Pulling this annoying stunt is one of the ways your car gets back at you for all the abuse it takes.

8. First-aid kit. Pick this up in a discount drugstore or an auto-supply store. You'll be surprised how often it comes in handy.

9. Jumper cables. I can't count the times I've gotten jump-started after I drained my battery by leaving my lights on or gave some other poor sucker a jump start. This is another one of those things that should be in every car and you should know how to use. (Check the instructions in the package.)

10. Duct tape. This is super strong gray tape two or three inches wide. It can be used to wrap a blown coolant hose—if you have it and use a little common sense to keep from getting burned or melting down your engine. Keep in mind that blown coolant hoses rank as

one of the two or three most common reasons for breaking down in the middle of nowhere.

Checklist for Car Survival

1. Don't play road games. Let the nut on the road have all the road he wants—you can't win with a crazy and you are risking more lives than your own.
2. Don't yell back or flip the bird at anyone—let the classless jerks get it off with their mouths—it's all they have. Remember, words and birds can't hurt you, but sticks and stones—and guns—can.
3. Don't honk your horn except in an emergency. That's what it's for.
4. Lock your door while still getting into your car—not after you get seated. The few seconds' difference may save your life.
5. If you get out of the car to go into a store, leaving family members in the car, take your keys with you and lock your car doors. (Never leave a small child alone in the car.)
6. If you're buying a new car, be sure and get the remote locking-unlocking feature.
7. When walking to your car, keep your remote entry in hand.
8. Park tactically—give as much concern about your tender skin as you do about getting parking lot rash on your doors.

9. When pumping gas, try to park close to the cashier.

10. If you're in an accident at night or you get "bumped" and you believe your safety is at risk, do not pull over. Signal the driver to follow you to a well-lighted area. If the driver won't follow you and you have a car phone, call 911 or drive to the nearest phone at a well-lighted, active business. Leaving the scene of an accident is a hit-and-run, so only do this if you believe your life is in danger.

11. Know the basics of how to change a flat tire. You may have to if you're in an isolated area.

18

Security at Work

Homicide is the leading cause of death for women in the workplace. It is second only to motor vehicle accidents as the cause of death for men.

Nearly 1 million individuals become victims of violent crime in the workplace each year.

In addition, there are 2 million personal thefts and 200,000 car thefts each year in a work environment.

—US Department of Justice,
Bureau of Justice Statistics

Violence in the workplace has become as common as on our streets. While some jobs are inherently risky—anywhere money is handled—another type of violence is occurring with greater frequency: berserkers who crack from stress and come to work with guns and relieve their pain by killing their coworkers.

The worst workplace horror story I have ever heard took place in one of the states west of the Mississippi. Robbers entered a record store and forced the employees into the basement. After assaulting them, they made them drink some sort of caustic drain cleaner. The father of one of the employees, wondering why his son had not come home from work, went to the store and was also murdered.

It happened a long time ago and I don't know why this story stuck with me. And I don't know what I would do if someone pointed a gun at me and told me I would have to drink an acid that would turn my insides to mush. Hopefully, I will never be in that position. Hopefully, the perpetrators are burning in hell.

Fortunately this sort of nightmare is not an everyday occurrence. Unfortunately, murder and other crime in the workplace are. Obviously working at places that handle *money* increases your chance of being a victim of a crime. Working at places that handle money at *night* further increases the odds. And working at places that handle money at night and that are located near *freeway on-ramps* makes the odds go up even more because easy-freeway-access locations are often chosen by robbers for getaways. Combine working at night, handling money in a location near a freeway, and a low-income area, and your odds shoot up astronomically.

People don't always have a choice as to where they work, but if there is a choice, do a little thinking about it. Play the *Dollars vs. Life* game. If the risk of working at that particular location is worth it, go for it.

And crime happens everywhere. My wife has had her computer stolen off of her desk by fellow employees in a secured building at a large corporation.

On the seventh floor of a building in one of the high-rent districts of the world (Beverly Hills), my secretary stepped out of the photocopy room and found a man behind her desk. She yelled at the man, and he rushed out the door and into a stairway, taking her purse with him. A purse snatcher in Beverly Hills? In a building that has guards on the main floor?

Another terrible statistic is the rising number of workplace robberies which end up in violence. Robbers too often casually kill the clerks and customers in stores. Often in full sight of video cameras without the slightest concern that they are being recorded.

There is nothing we can do as individuals to affect the nationwide epidemic of assaults in the workplace from criminals off of the streets, but there are a couple of things that we can do to reduce our chances of becoming victims.

I am not going to tell you not to work in a place that handles money. People work where they can get a job.

However, if you do have to work in a place that handles money, and especially if you work at night, talk to your employer about security, perhaps getting a security expert to design a plan for the business.

One factor that helps is visibility. Remove signs, posters, or other objects that block the employees' view of people approaching the location. Another is secured parking. Parking out in the back alley that has faint light is not a safe and sane procedure. Neither is having a trash bin or a break area in a back alley. Fences and lights work wonders to help make such areas safer.

Video cameras are something of a deterrent despite the number of crazies willing to smile at the camera and kill while their picture is being taken. If it's any satisfaction, there is more chance of catching and convicting the criminal that killed you if the action is caught on video.

A silent-alarm system is even more valuable. It usually involves a button near the cash register or desk that you press with your hand or foot. When you have the chance. It is not clever to reach for the button when someone has a gun on you.

Another factor is simply not to get lazy about security. Think it out and have a plan about what you will do when someone shoves a gun in your face. If it is just a matter of handing over the cash, that's easy enough. But more and more frequently the criminal is killing everyone in sight. That's when a silent alarm comes in handy. When someone walks in and points a gun at you, the last thing you need is for someone to hit a button that sets off a noisy alarm. That is likely to get you killed.

There is another philosophy about getting robbed—some people believe the best thing is not to have an alarm because they may get caught in a cross fire when the police arrive.

It is a judgment call, but with the rise of violent robberies, I would opt for a system where I knew the authorities were being summoned. And if I am going to be killed, it would be a relief to know that there was a better chance of the killer being caught because the police were notified while the robbery was going down.

Some people seem to have the gods smiling at them. One of my neighbors owned a store in a ghetto for years. He was held up at gunpoint seven times and never got a scratch. But what are the odds of that happening? Would you bet your life on seven robberies and no harm?

Surviving Maniacs at Your Job

There was a time in this world when, unless you worked in a bank or had a night job at a gas station, there was very little chance of you meeting up with violence in the workplace and that violence came from strangers. Unfortunately, too many people suffering too much stress and a proliferation of guns has led to an array of violence in the workplace and the perpetrators are coworkers.

In nineteen incidents of deadly violence perpetrated by co-workers on the job that I tracked in one metro area, ten (over half of all the incidents) took place at *government* facilities.

Four of the ten government-facility incidents occurred at post offices, making working at the post office something akin safety wise to working the graveyard shift guarding an ATM machine in a high-crime area.

Another "trend" has been killings at plants, factories, and other blue-collar facilities. While such violence does not occur with the frequency of street crime, it does happen too often—one automobile plant had *two* killings in *two* years.

In the 1990s in each of the largest metropolitan areas of America, there has been a "multiple-killings" incident by a berserk worker almost every year. Four or five deaths per incident with more wounded are not uncommon.

There was a time when a workplace killing would make national news, but they happen too frequently now to generate that sort of coverage. The shocking thing is that violence in the workplace is escalating nationally, that the reported cases of violence exceed a million a year with deaths arising from violence amounting to several thousand each year.

Many workplace problems cannot be avoided—a jealous husband arrives at his wife's work and kills her, her lover, the security guard, and whoever else is in the line of fire. By the time a berserker arrives at work with a gun ready to kill, it's going to be hard to defuse the situation because the violence erupts so quickly and unexpectedly and the perpetrator may be too crazy to deal with.

In that scenario, the wife carried her victim's mentality onto the job and made the workplace the wrong place and time for her coworkers.

The violence that is taken to the workplace by a jealous spouse is almost impossible for an employer to control because the berserker is not part of the work environment. However, the violence erupting from workers and customers does stem from the work environment, and some of it is manageable.

Other than using metal detectors and heavily armed guards, an impractical way to deal with tens of millions of workers, about the only way to try and deal with potential violence at the workplace is to develop programs that educate the employees as to symptoms that can lead to workplace violence and have professionals attempt to deal with the affected employee before it gets out of hand.

But expecting managers, who may in fact be the cause, or at least the focal point of the angry employee's ire, to diffuse an emotional crisis may range from the improbable to the impossible. A more reasonable approach would be to have professional counselors deal with the situation.

The first problem is identifying where the violence might initiate from. A berserker does not give the opportunity of defusing his irrational anger by announcing his intention of returning to work with an assault weapon and killing the people who have been giving him a bad time or are responsible for layoffs.

Notice I use "him" as the gender for a berserker? A person who brings violence to the workplace can be any sex, race or age, but the following factors have created a perhaps oversimplified "prototype" of the type of person who has brought violence to the workplace:

1. The culprit is most commonly a *man*
2. Has a pending disciplinary problem, a bad review, and has been (or is about to be) terminated

3. Has been a disciplinary problem previously
4. Tends to be alienated from fellow employees
5. Is likely a gun owner
6. Is in the throes of emotional breakdown

Daniel Marsden, a Long Beach, California, plastics company quality-control inspector, fit the pattern perfectly. Right down to owning a gun.

Marsden, thirty-eight years old, was described by coworkers as a "quiet man" who was thought of by his coworkers as a bit "strange."

He ate his lunch alone, sitting in his car a couple of blocks from the plant, and after work he would sit in the car for another couple of hours, just staring into space.

He appeared to wear the same white cotton shirt and polyester pants to work each day. He had been employed at the plant for about eighteen months.

The incident that precipitated a killing spree began over what would normally have been a "routine" incident, a minor argument that Marsden interpreted as everyone talking behind his back.

After the argument, Marsden walked out to his car and got a gun. He walked into the plant office and shot a thirty-three-year-old woman working at a computer terminal. He turned and shot another employee who was standing nearby staring in disbelief.

Marsden then made his way through the plant, calmly walking along, firing his 9mm semiautomatic handgun, firing at people at random, shooting three more people, including a salesman for a company that supplies parts for the plant. He shot a sixth person, hitting a man in the back as the man ran out of the plant and into the parking lot.

Then Marsden went to his car and drove away. About an hour later he got out of his car next to where two people

213

were using a pay phone in front of a store. He pointed the gun at one of the women, and said, "This is my last day of life."

He stuck the gun in his mouth and pulled the trigger.

Including Marsden, the incident left seven victims—three dead and four wounded.

Could the incident with Marsden have been avoided? No one will ever know because the person with the answer stuck a gun in his mouth, but what strikes me about the situation is how well Marsden fit the "problem" prototype. It is obvious that Marsden was suffering a mental disorder. That should have been obvious even before he grabbed his gun. Coworkers called his behavior "strange" and "weird." He was alienated from other workers and was a disciplinary problem.

One thing probably true was his paranoia that people were talking about him behind his back. Few of us are going to walk up to the guy and say, "Hey, man, you're nuts," but it would be a common reaction (and a very human and natural reaction) to speak about him to other employees when he was out of the range of hearing. *The guy was nuts.*

How to defuse a Marsden without trampling on a host of his rights (not to mention common decency and a lawsuit) is a hairy problem.

We don't have all of the information about Marsden before us, and one critical piece of missing information is whether people at the plant knew he was a gun owner, or, even more significantly, that he kept a gun in his car.

I am not sure where you draw the line to deal with the Marsdens in this world. There are plenty of them around who would not hurt a fly, but if I was an employee at a plant and I observed that a fellow employee was wigging out, and I knew the guy kept a gun out in his car, I think I would try to get management to get help for this guy or start looking at the want ads myself.

Marsden perfectly fit the prototype, but the problem with prototypes is that they are too often *stereotypes*. Look at the FBI "profiling" techniques that have been so successful at finding serial killers and terrorists. The profile blew up in the FBI's face when they tried to hang an innocent man with the Atlanta bombing.

A male employee who never got along with fellow employees and has been terminated for a history of disciplinary problems constitutes a significant percentage of the millions of men terminated every year. Not to mention that many of these millions of men own guns.

A more accurate denominator of the type of berserker who might get a gun and bring it back to work is someone who has broken down emotionally under the pressures of life and imagines that the root of all of his or her problems stem from people at work.

I believe that *emotional breakdown* and *gun ownership* are the real keys to "profiling" a berserker. Not every berserker will fit into the profile, and conversely, only a tiny percent of those who fit the profile are berserkers, but at least we can consider gun ownership and emotional disturbance, in combination with the other factors, as red flags that we should notice.

People react differently to stress and problems in their life. Some of us hide in a corner and lick our wounds, others "project" the cause of their problems on other people (how many times in juvenile court have I heard Mom and Dad say it wasn't Johnny's fault, it was the kids he ran around with). The truth about gun ownership and emotional disturbance is that more people "murder" themselves with guns than they murder other people.

Some of the people who project do it to an extreme, focusing on a single person or a group of people whom they believe are the cause of their problems. They may be very verbal about it or the paranoia may fester inside them until their soul rots and their emotions melt down.

Obviously, for every berserker who acts out his problems with violence, there are many thousands of disturbed persons who do not. The problem is how to deal with even the small potential for violence within the bounds of laws and decency.

The safe and sane approach is to develop an *awareness* that violence does visit the workplace and to develop *programs* to deal with that potential.

How to deal with a potential "berserker" involves an incredible array of legal, moral, ethical, psychological, and humanitarian problems. Programs should include training employees on how to identify potential problems and training management to deal with the reported problems without overreacting, ruining careers, making matters worse, or generating legal action.

What we would not want is a group of employees pointing the finger at another employee, a sort of workplace lynch mob, saying that the person is a danger (if he isn't convinced of conspiracies before he got the finger pointed at him, he sure as hell will be afterward).

What we do want are programs to make employees, at all levels, from the sweepers to the movers and shakers, more sensitive to the issue of workplace violence, to develop an awareness that violence is a potential.

Programs to identify and deal with potential problems are best left to professionals. But an *awareness* is something each of us should have. We live in a very stressful society and when people crack under that stress and begin acting strange or confrontational, the worst thing we can do is to fuel the fires by *reacting* with more confrontation.

The situation is not unlike challenging some nut on the highway who goes berserk over a trivial auto incident. You can further aggravate the situation by rubbing salt into the jerk's raw emotions, or you can try to ride out the crisis by not turning a potentially violent nut into a really kill-crazy one.

There is an old expression about oil soothing troubled waters—these are the times to be oil and not the catalyst that turns anger into violence.

Bomb Threats at Work

Bombs and the threat of being bombed are harsh realities in our world. Bombs have done horrible damage on a large scale in major cities. The Unibomber and copycats have instituted reigns of terror through the mail.

As an individual, these are some things you should know.

A "bomb" in this context will not look like our mental image of a bomb. It can look like anything. If it is delivered through the mail, its appearance is likely to be that of an ordinary package.

What about all of the other ordinary packages you deal with—how do you separate those from the others? You may not be able to, but there are a couple of things that might separate them from the others.

First, you may recognize the sender of most of your packages while the bomb package may have a strange name or even no name or return address. It may have a foreign address (but don't expect it to be conveniently postmarked Baghdad or Beirut).

Second, some of the bombs sent in the mail have been a little more crudely or sloppily wrapped, as opposed to the packages sent out by reputable business entities.

Third, if you work at a company that engenders bomb threats by its very nature (government agencies, abortion clinics, defense contractors, etc.) you should be a little more cautious, but keep in mind that the Unibomber targeted individuals who sometimes had only the most tenuous link to his grudge against the world.

There are bomb threats—and then there are actual bombs. Sometimes the threat is made just to disrupt the company it is directed toward. But all bomb threats have to be taken seriously.

They have to be reported immediately to the police. And, depending on the nature of the threat and the nature of the facility, an immediate decision has to be made as to whether the threat is to be ignored or the premises evacuated.

Personally, if I am in a building in which there has been a bomb threat, I will evacuate immediately. I am not going to wait around while someone whose usual job is to count paper clips decides whether it is safe for me to remain in the building. It's *my* life, and I will take the ultimate responsibility for protecting it. I am not talking about running in panic—I'm talking about being *expedient*.

19

Traveling Safely

Criminals know where, when, and how to find tourists. And they know exactly what to say to them. They're nice. They'll ask you where you're from—and then jack you up for your wallet, camera, and jewelry.

—Fieldings, *The World's Most Dangerous Places*

People traveling have a greater chance of being victims of crime than when they are at home because criminals all over the world prey on them. Too many people make victims of themselves by leaving their personal safety at home. People leave their cars at home protected by car alarms, with their houses protected by house alarms . . . and turn their safety over to the minimum-wage night clerk at a motel who will be a hundred yards away and sleeping when they face an intruder in their room. Government studies show that security preparations for traveling, ranging from where to sit on an airplane to which floor you select in a hotel or motel, can save your life.

The worst sin people commit while traveling is falling under the unconscious delusion that because they are only visiting, they are somehow impervious to the dangers of the city or the area they are in.

It's not that most people don't worry about things being stolen from their hotel room—people make sure to stuff their money, passport, and credit cards into their pockets to "safeguard" them from hotel thieves and proceed to walk out into areas of the city at night that the locals would not be caught *alive* in.

I know because I have been one of those unconscious fools. I have driven a motor home into remote areas of the jungles of the Yucatan and had *federales* armed with machine guns invite themselves in, have taken off from Cairo in a taxi with two women aboard, up the Nile to Luxor and across the desert to the Red Sea without a thought that a religious fanatic might like to put a bullet in my head (actually, all I ran into was dozens of wonderful people who treated us like honored guests, even when we were forced to stay in a pink whorehouse in one town because the hotels were full and had to eat in the marketplace because there were no restaurants); and we've wandered at night through a couple of dozen foreign cities without a thought that we might be in danger.

We came through all of it safely although we were pick-pocketed by Gypsies in Rome and had a wallet stolen (as I mentioned earlier, I lost nothing to the Gypsies because *I* had read the guidebooks and was prepared), my wife's purse was stolen in a very nice restaurant in a good neighborhood in Manhattan, a traveling companion's wallet was stolen at the train station at quaint historical York in Merry Ole England (if you had to be robbed this is the place because the police are so bloody polite and remorseful—it was almost worth it for our friend to have *her* wallet stolen just to experience old-fashioned police concern), and we had someone try to break into our motel room near the New Jersey Turnpike . . . unfortunately at a time when we were occupying the rooms.

The loss to the Gypsies and the train-station thief are obviously losses usually unique to traveling. Both losses could have been avoided had we all been more security conscious. My wife, who has led a much more sheltered life than me, had to get burned a couple of times before she got security conscious. In the purse incident, we were having dinner at a nice restaurant in a nice area of Manhattan with nice people—the restaurant was a bit dark and crowded and my wife and a friend (yeah, Carol, who had a wallet stolen in England and Rome) slung their purses over the backs of their chairs. I might add that they both prefer very small purses on long straps. There was a minor disturbance in another part of the restaurant as someone who had come in from the street tried to take a reserved table. We turned to look and shortly thereafter discovered the purses were gone.

My wife now makes sure her purse is glued to her in restaurants. And our friend? Her wallet tumbled out of her purse afterward in a taxi in Chicago, she didn't ask for a taxi receipt, didn't note the driver's name or number, and the *next day* her credit cards were used in Paris . . . France. (Worse things have happened to this lovely, intelligent woman than losing her wallet, and she is still completely oblivious to anything concerning personal security. My lectures go in one ear and out the other. The sole benefit we have gained from traveling with her is that thieves are more likely to hone in on her than us).

What sort of things does a security-conscious person do to ensure their safety and that of their family when traveling?

The main thing is simply to stay security conscious while

you're gawking at all of the sights or hurrying up to wait for trains, planes, and rental cars.

I mentioned the problem with mind-sets earlier—like being impervious to driving through a violent ghetto because you're in your employer's car. Or not thinking about walking out to a dark parking lot because it's an employee parking lot.

Traveling involves the same sort of mind-set.

The first thing you should do is give some thought to security *before* you leave home.

Start with what you are taking with you in terms of valuables.

I'm sure you've seen on educational TV shows stories of women in third-world countries literally carrying the family wealth around their neck and on their wrists. I'm reminded of that every time I travel and I see men and women wearing expensive watches and gold necklaces.

If there is any time *not* to wear expensive jewelry, it's when you are traveling and at your most vulnerable.

Keep that thought in your mind while you decide what not to take on your trip: You will be at your most vulnerable. You will be leaving personal effects in hotels and motels that strangers with keys will enter while you are away. You will be eating out all of the time and spending half of your life lost in big cities in rental cars. The other half of the time you will be gawking at some incredible piece of ancient architecture while a pickpocket is taking your money, credit cards, and . . . your passport. Ever stand in line at an American embassy to get a temporary passport?

Expensive watches and jewelry do not travel well unless you get limo treatment at the airport and around town, stay only in the best hotels, and never leave the hotel except in an armored car.

Leave your nice watches, heirlooms, expensive wedding

rings, and gold chains home because they are neons for grab-and-dash thieves.

And don't travel with a great deal of cash. Today, with credit cards and ATM machines in almost universal use, you don't need a great deal of cash.

Leave home all of the credit cards you will not use. I take *one* bank card (Visa or MasterCard) and my American Express Card. My wife takes a *different* bank card than me and an AMEX card with a different number. That way, if one of us loses a wallet and we have to call in and cancel credit cards, we still have usable cards.

Don't take your checkbook with you for an out-of-state trip. It would be rare to be able to get anyone to accept a check out of state and it's just something else to lose. I carry one *unsigned* check on trips for use in case of . . . of . . . I'm not sure why I carry a blank check since no one would cash it anyway, but I just do it. Maybe someday I'll find myself in a jungle outpost and they won't take a credit card, won't take cash, will *only take a check.* Maybe they have a tribal fetish for checks. Okay, maybe I'm just paranoid. But I won't leave home without one blank check in my wallet.

Separate your cash into two portions: Carry the money you need on a daily basis and one of the credit cards in your wallet. Put the other credit cards, your passport, and the bulk of your cash in a money belt (you can use a conventional belly type or one around your ankle). If you want to get really clever, someone told me he carries a large number of small bills with a large bill on top in a dummy wallet to be able to hand it over to a thief if necessary—his theory, like mine, is that a pleased thief doesn't kill as often, and this way you can get robbed and not have it ruin your trip.

If you are traveling overseas, make photocopies of your passport. Leave one copy back home with a friend or relative who can fax it if you need it, and carry the other copy with you because it will come in handy if the original is lost or stolen. If you do not have your passport number when you go to the American consulate or embassy to report the loss, you will have delays having a passport issued—and you can't go home without one!

Hotels tend to be fairly safe places to leave valuables. But with a computer, which has data on it that is impossible to replace, I am paranoid as hell. If I have to leave the computer in my room, I slip it far enough under the bed so the maid's vacuum cleaner won't hit it—and to make sure I won't be 40,000 feet high and half a continent away before I realize my computer's back at the hotel, I leave my plane ticket with my computer. (I know what you're thinking—someday a thieving hotel maid is going to be 40,000 feet high and half a continent away in the Concorde playing solitaire on my laptop by the time I look under the bed.)

Rental cars are also a problem. The shocking violence against tourists leaving Florida airports in rental cars has gotten a lot of publicity, but to a lesser extent rental cars attract thieves all over the world because tourists tend to be more careless and thus more vulnerable than the locals.

If any of the evidence that you're in a rental car is removable, take it off (a decal on the bumper might be removable with a pen knife). When you make purchases or carry luggage, always make sure the items are placed out of sight in the trunk—don't leave anything on the seat. If you don't leave your camera in the trunk, at least leave it under the front seat or at the foot of the front passenger seat where it may be hard to see from the outside.

Women should not carry bulky purses. It's okay to carry a bulky shoulder bag for purchases, but don't dump your purse or wallet in it because the pickpockets frequent the same places tourists do and bulky purses and bags are easy to slip a hand into. Fanny packs are sometimes cut open by pickpockets and purse straps sliced. Keeping your purse dangling more toward the front side of your body helps avoid these types of thieves.

When shopping in tourist places and you need your hands free, carry your purse over your shoulder and strapped across your chest. That way you only have your shopping bag to deal with and you are less likely to leave your purse behind or have it stolen because you've set it down while handling merchandise. Men should never carry a wallet in a pocket that does not either zip or button.

Check out hotel accommodations made from afar before committing to them. This is pretty easy to do by going to the local bookstore and looking up the hotel in the travel-book section. If you or a friend belong to an auto club, you can check it out in their publications.

If you can't check out the hotel in travel books, call the hotel and try to get a straight answer about the quality of the hotel and the safety of the location from a clerk. Every time I did this I got an honest answer.

If you suspect you are not getting the straight dope, ask the hotel clerk for a restaurant recommendation, get the number from the clerk, and call the restaurant—tell them exactly what you are doing and ask about the hotel and the area. Transcontinental and international calls are not expensive anymore, especially when you consider that spending a few dollars on calls might save you much misery.

Another piece of advice—if you are not an experienced traveler, don't stay in places you can't check out in travel books.

Once in a restaurant in Bath, England, we struck up a conversation with people at the next table and a young British woman mentioned she was making a trip to Los Angeles. We lived in the city at the time and we asked her where she would be staying. A travel agent had booked her into a motel in Hollywood that I was familiar with because I passed it coming off the freeway many times. I told the woman that the motel was in a drug-infested area—not that that description doesn't fit most of Hollywood, but this motel had another terrible aspect: In order to see what little there is to see in Hollywood, the young woman would have had to walk mean streets to get to Hollywood Boulevard.

What's a mean street? Streets that are not crowded, not well lit, not well patrolled by the police, and the inhabitants look at you like you're going to be the source of their next fix. The motel had a rating from a national service. I assume the rooms were clean and the facilities decent and safe. That means I will be safe in my room, but I don't go on vacation to stay barricaded in my room.

In a city like New York, where taxis are at every corner, a decent hotel in a less-than-respectable neighborhood is no big deal. In Los Angeles, where Hollywood is plopped down in one of the worst areas, it is hell because the city doesn't have widespread taxi service available and public buses in the Hollywood area are "high-crime areas" all to themselves.

Locations can be tricky. When staying in Manhattan, I prefer to take a respectable hotel in an area that will be busy at night—places like Times Square (where half the street trash in the city hang out), Lincoln Center, Central Park West and Central Park South—rather than an even better hotel on a street lined with high-rise business buildings. Why? Because places like Times Square are filled with people day and night (some of those people are even cops) and the odds of someone pulling a gun or knife on you is slight—but walking back from the theater district or financial district at night to a hotel in a business district can be scary *because all of those high-rise business buildings filled with thousands of people in the daytime are dark and empty and there's no one on the streets except muggers and rapists waiting for you to return to your hotel down those dark and lonely canyons.*

While the above may be a slight exaggeration, the scariest walks I ever took were when I stayed in one of the most famous hotels in Manhattan and discovered that the hotel was in the heart of the commercial district that became a ghost town at night—all I saw walking back were the feet of homeless people sleeping in doorways.

Today I would take a taxi back to the hotel, but in those days I was too embarrassed to have a taxi take me a few blocks. Now I don't let a little thing like being embarrassed get me in the path of muggers.

Stay off the subways and buses at night, *anywhere* in the world. Pay the extra money and take taxis. Subways in big cities are safe in the daytime during workdays, less safe on weekends, and not safe at all at night—anywhere.

When traveling, vehicle rest stops are another place I try to avoid. To use a bathroom, I prefer stopping at fast-food restaurants rather than rest stops. (Gas stations are usually disgusting in terms of bathrooms and many fast-food restaurants are getting that way, making you wonder how clean their kitchens are.) A crowded rest stop on a holiday weekend is tolerable in terms of security—but who the hell wants to use the bathroom in one, anyway?

You are safe in almost any decent hotel. Most hotels today have doors that you can lock from the inside so not even a maid can get in. Once in your room, always set the inner lock and don't open the door unless you know exactly who is outside. If someone claiming to be hotel personnel wants in, call the front desk and verify why the person is at your door. Don't be intimidated about calling—there is nothing wrong with being cautious.

I always note where the fire escapes are, too. I'm not so paranoid that I carry mountain-climbing gear to rappel down the side in case of fire, but I at least check where the nearest stairways are on my way to my room because the next time I try to find a fire escape the hallway may be full of smoke.

After settling into my room, I take a trip down the corridor to check out the fire escapes more thoroughly. I also try to get a room on as low a level as possible above the first floor (unless there is a great view—I admit I am a sucker and usually willing to sacrifice some security for a great view).

I always check out the possible escape routes in my hotel room by walking over to the window and estimating how many legs I would break if I had to jump because of a fire. To be sure, the rooms are usually so high I would be a splattered bug if I had to jump, but there have been occasions when there are ledges to crawl along and other roofs near enough to break a leg or two jumping onto. (Has anyone ever really escaped a hotel fire by tying sheets and blankets into a rope?)

The safest bet for hotels is to get a room between the second and seventh floor because fire-department equipment is rarely able to go higher. Don't bet on fire-department equipment going that high in many third-world countries (don't count on fire equipment in third-world countries, period).

And keep in mind that in much of the world, they start *numbering* floors from the *second* floor—so what we call the first floor is the ground floor and what we call the second floor is their *first* floor.

If you are traveling in the third world and stay in a hotel that is not a name brand, you might also ask a little about the hotel before making a reservation. I once reserved a third-floor room . . . and 12,000 miles later when we arrived I discovered that the *third* floor I reserved was the *seventeenth* floor because the hotel was at the top of an office building (the lobby was on the ground floor and the rooms started fourteen floors up—but having a room from which we could see the heart of Cairo turned out to be wonderful).

In checking out the fire escape in my seventeenth-floor room, I discovered *the fire escapes were kept locked for security reasons.*

You may have seen in some hotels a fire alarm where you break the glass and pull the handle. What *my* seventeenth floor corridor had was a *key* to the fire-escape door—the idea was that you broke the glass and grabbed the key and then ran like hell down seventeen flights.

I carry one of those tiny but powerful little flashlights in my luggage in case I need it in the middle of the night or have to evacuate a hotel when the power is off. I was once in a high-rise when the electric power and emergency backup system failed, and it was hell finding a stairway and inching down seven stories in the dark.

Most of the above regards air travel to major cities. However, most trips people take are by car, usually their own, and they stay at low-rise motels rather than hotels. These trips involve some different security concerns.

Decent motels are generally safe, just as decent hotels are. But in general, motels require a little more security concern than hotels because the rooms are lower to the ground and thus more accessible.

I prefer a room on the *second* floor or above in a motel because street-level rooms are easier for criminals to access. Ground-floor motel rooms (and hotel rooms) are particularly unsafe if they open onto a beach, street, or alley.

I admit that I have taken a ground-floor room in a good hotel because the room opened onto the beach. The only excuse I have is that the view was great. But I made sure the sliding glass door had a double lock on it, and when I went to bed at night I leaned an aerosol can on the door handle so if the door opened the can would fall and make noise.

In the many dozens of motels I have stayed in, I doubt if one out of ten had security locks on room windows. To the contrary, while motel-room doors tend to be the type you can double lock from the inside, the windows in front and in the bathroom are usually sliders on inexpensive aluminum frames. I commonly find that the windows cannot even be securely locked because they have been installed so sloppily. I rarely find any sort of effective lock on a motel window even when the factory lock works.

If I don't trust the window, I take aerosol cans (like hair spray and shaving lotion) and stand them against the window so the pile will fall if anyone tries to enter. I have seen extension rods you can buy in travel stores to block windows, but I don't think I would ever remember to carry it with me—or if I did, I'd probably forget it in the first window I stuck it in.

Having a second-story room helps with the window problem. Locking the windows if they are lockable also helps. I find an amazing number of motel-room windows unlocked when I check in; it doesn't seem to be something on a maid's checklist.

I do not stay at dumpy motels, period. Cheap and shabby motels have frequently been the scene of break-ins, thefts, and rapes. Motel doors tend to be flimsy, and it doesn't take much for someone to put a shoulder to the door and be in your room with little noise.

One of my clients was raped in a cheap hotel room. She woke up to find a man climbing on top of her. He had rented the room before and kept the key after he left. I would rather pay the extra money for a better motel or drive on to find one I'd feel safe in than put myself and my family in harm's way to save a few bucks.

In most motels, I will wedge a chair against the door before I go to bed. A rubber door stopper is also good, but I never remember to bring one (although I keep one in the utility box of my car just for that purpose—I just have never remembered it was there when I needed it).

You rarely find a chair that fits perfectly under the door handle to make it hard to force open the door. But any chair may slow down or scare off someone by offering some physical resistance while I am asleep. I also rig up my own little "burglar alarm" for the door by placing an aerosol can on the door handle and leaning it against the frame, or on the top of the chair and leaning it against the handle, so if the door opens, the can falls. (This is similar to how I "alarm" the windows—if you think I'm a paranoid nut, keep reading and I'll tell you about how paranoid our own government is.)

If you travel with a laptop computer or expensive camera gear, take special care at airport metal detectors—thieves acting in concert watch you put your expensive equipment on the conveyer belt, then one thief hurries through the metal detector and the other steps in and plugs up the line by having something metallic in his/her pocket. While you're waiting for the line to clear, the other thief has walked away with your three-thousand-dollar computer.

Camera bags can also be the target of conveyer-belt thieves. My friend who carries a dummy wallet stuffed with small bills also camouflages his camera by putting the camera bag in a larger carry-on rather than tempting fate by advertising his expensive camera.

Be careful about what you put into your check-in luggage. Besides the possibility of airline baggage employees stealing, having had airlines lose my check-in luggage several times (always to be found later), I don't trust my most important items in check-in. I always put in my carry-on luggage critical items that will be difficult to replace: eyeglasses, contact-lens case, contact-lens fluid, hotel and other reservation documents, tickets, travel maps, Swiss Army knife, small flashlight, medication, copy of my passport, and the like.

Because my eye contacts are easy to lose, I carry a spare set. If I was on medication, I would take a copy of the prescription. (You probably think I should be on Prozac.)

I can't tell you what *not* to put in your check-in luggage, but I can give you a simple rule of thumb: If it is going to ruin your trip if it's lost or stolen, don't put it in your check-in luggage. I know that the loss of most of your clothing in a check-in bag will play hell on your trip, but clothes can be replaced en route—you may not be able to replace your glasses or medication quickly at any expense (although you may get someone at home to overnight the item to you).

Some people carry a spare set of underwear in case their baggage is lost. My theory is that type of stuff is easy to buy, easy to wash if it can't be bought, and I'd just as soon use the space for something irreplaceable.

When you book an air flight, get a *nonstop* flight rather than what the airlines euphemistically call a *direct* flight. A direct flight is one that makes a stopover. Why do you want to avoid a stopover? Because most air crashes occur during *takeoff* or *landing,* by adding another takeoff and landing you increase your risk (also takeoff and landing crashes are about the only *survivable* crashes; it doesn't do much good to make plans for a crash that starts 40,000 feet up).

Throw in some nasty winter weather and you increase your risk even more.

Does it cost a few dollars more for a nonstop flight? Sometimes. But I'd rather spend the price of a meal dining out than take the added risk of another takeoff and landing.

I prefer an aisle seat on an airplane for several reasons. One is that I hate crawling over people when I get up to go to the bathroom or stretch my legs. Another reason is that in case of emergency, you can get out faster. You are a trapped rat in a window seat. A cooked goose if the plane is on fire.

Another factor to consider when deciding where to sit on a plane is that the tail is sometimes unhinged and left intact in *survivable* crashes—so it's not a bad place to sit. Definitely better than first-class at the front of the plane, which may take the major impact on crashing. I usually try to get a seat by the exits over the wings or other bulkheads. The wing portion of the plane is the strongest portion and thus the most likely to stay together in a *survivable* crash—but it is also where the fuel is stored.

Thinking about where you are going to sit, thinking about where the exits are if the plane crashes, about how the life vest works (people have died in *survivable* crashes because they blew up their life vest before getting out of the plane—when the plane went under, they couldn't get out because their life vests were inflated!), keeping your seat belt fastened even when the warning sign is not on, all create one thing that might keep you alive—an awareness of your surroundings and a contingency plan so that if the plane does crash and you have only seconds to save your life, you don't waste them by having to think about what you should do.

Before you decide to go the fatalistic route and say the hell with it, you wouldn't be able to survive a plane crash anyway, keep the following stunning statistic from the Federal Aviation Administration in mind: Almost three out of every four people who die in survivable plane crashes die *after* the plane has come to a complete halt on the ground.

Our Government Is Just
As Paranoid As I Am

After reading this you probably think I'm a little weird, probably wondering if I need something stronger than Prozac—rigging up noisemakers to ward off intruders in my motel room, requesting lower-level hotel rooms, insisting on nonstop flights, etc. If so, you can add the *United States Department of State* to the weird category.

In one of their pamphlets about security and traveling, they recommend not only putting a chair up against the door, but rigging up a "burglar alarm" with the use of two glass ashtrays and a water glass: You put one ash tray on the floor next to the door, put the glass on top and put the second ashtray on top of the glass. If someone opens the door, the pile of glass falls over.

I like my aerosol cans just as well, but after reading the State Department's advice I am considering the water glass–ashtray trick, although finding a room with ashtrays has gotten tougher with no-smoking rooms prevalent in hotels nowadays.

Reading the State Department pamphlet also gave me a real boost because other security measures I take while traveling are also recommended by the government. They advise their employees to book *nonstop* flights, to request *lower-level* hotel rooms, to check out the *fire escapes,* to check the *locks* on doors and windows, to keep the *inner locks* attached while in their room, to *photocopy their passports,* and a dozen other things I have been doing for years.

After I read the pamphlet, I ran through the house yelling to my wife, "See! See! I'm not the only crazy one! The government's crazy, too!"

In all seriousness, before you kick the State Department

advice out of bed, don't forget that these people may be the world's most experienced travelers.

Additionally, never discount the benefits of being prepared for any emergency, even one as rare as an air crash. The following is a quote from a United States Department of Transportation publication:

> After an air accident, the National Transportation Safety Board always talks to survivors to try and learn why they were able to make it through safely. They have discovered that, as a rule, it does help to be prepared. *Avoiding serious injury isn't just a matter of luck; it's also a matter of being informed and thinking ahead.*

When you walk onto a plane, into a crowded nightclub or movie theater, check into a motel or hotel, give at least as much thought to your safety as you would crossing a street in front of your house. At least look to see where the exits are before you need them with fire licking at your tush.

Travel, Terrorism, and Kidnapping

With terrorism on the rise, there are some fundamental points you should know.

While we usually think of terrorist attacks in terms of bombings of planes and buildings, many of the attacks are in terms of kidnappings. The average tourist going to a foreign country is not in significant danger of being kidnapped. Wealthy tourists who flaunt their money have a higher risk. These kidnappings happen in Europe as well as the third world.

Business people sent to work overseas, especially in third-world countries and the former Soviet bloc, have a risk, and these events happen much more frequently than terrorist bombings and get much less publicity. Any company sending personnel to these countries should have a kidnapping policy. If you are traveling to one of these countries on business or being transferred there, find out what the company policy is about paying ransom—i.e., when the kidnappers cut off one of your ears and send it to the company, will the company pay or let them filet you? You are taking a risk for the company by carrying their business overseas—if you can't pin them down to a particular position on kidnapping and you still want the assignment, ask them to provide an insurance policy that pays ransom.

I advise business people traveling to countries where there is a risk not to publicize their trip and only advise others of the travel plans on a need-to-know basis.

Here are some other tips about traveling and terrorism:

If your trip is solely within the United States and you fear a bomb in the bay of the airplane you will be flying in, you can gain a tiny edge by flying with an airline that serves only the continental United States because statistically, most terrorist attacks on planes have been on international flights.

If you are paranoid about flying anyway (as I am—despite flying thousands of miles each year), you can increase your chances of surviving an air crash by sitting near an exit and choosing an airline that has less aged planes than ones used by the discount and charter airlines. Of course, if the plane is the target of a terrorist bomb, the age of the plane is not going to make any difference. And the exit seat trick only works when there is a survivable crash . . .

When you travel outside the country, there is more chance of being a victim of terrorism. The fear is great enough that some people who visit the Holy Land have the customs officer stamp a blank sheet of paper rather than put the evidence in their passports that they have been to Israel and thus might be Jewish or a supporter of Hebrew causes.

When you travel in third-world areas, use some common sense. I have traveled off the beaten path in several third-world areas and found that the people I met were even nicer than the homegrown variety, but when I left the standard tourist areas I also left behind some of the security my tourist dollar buys (most countries try to make sure tourists do not get murdered because it is bad for business).

The State Department recommends its personnel take window seats rather than aisle seats on planes because people on the aisle are most likely to be considered victims in case of hijacking.

As long as plane crashes occur more frequently than airborne terrorist attacks, I will stick to an aisle seat.

Travel Checklist

1. Stay at decent hotels and motels. Don't put your life in jeopardy to save a few bucks. Check out the room and look over the territory before checking in. If you're not satisfied, move on.
2. At a hotel, locate the nearest fire escape *before* you need it. When you need it, it may be too smoky to locate.
3. Try for a second-story room at a motel—ground-floor rooms are more susceptible to break-ins.
4. Don't open the door for *anybody* unless you know why they are there. Call the front desk if there is any question at all. Talk through the door without opening it until you are

sure of who's outside—those chain guards on doors are usually a joke. Don't be intimidated just because someone on the other side of the door states they are with the hotel. Stall them while you call down to the front desk. If there is any question, have them send someone up immediately.

5. Avoid rest stops except when they are crowded. Then don't stop anyway.

6. In a major metropolitan area, a good hotel in a busy hot spot, even locations with street trash (where is downtown in a major metropolitan area free of street trash?) may be preferable to one that you have to walk dark and lonely streets to get back to.

7. Stay off of mass transportation at night and especially on weekends. The safest time (and most miserable in terms of comfort) is commute time. Don't try to save a few bucks and take the subway at night or hoof it across unfamiliar territory—spend a few bucks and take a taxi.

8. While driving (or even just sitting in your car) keep your doors locked.

9. If possible, take the rental-car decal off your rental car if you are going to be doing extensive traveling.

10. Don't leave valuables on your seats when you park.

11. Separate your cash into two portions—keep some in your wallet and the rest in a money belt.

12. Make a copy of your passport in case your passport is lost or stolen.

13. When you check into a motel room, check the windows and doors to make sure they are secure. At night, wedge a chair under the doorknob or against the door.
14. Watch your luggage at the airport; be aware of scams at the metal detectors.
15. Download your credit cards, expensive jewelry, and watches when you take a trip. You don't need that kind of extra baggage.
16. Carry your purse in front of you, over your shoulder and across your chest.
17. Make sure your car is equipped for emergency roadside situations.
18. Unless you are an experienced traveler, don't book accommodations that aren't rated in travel books.
19. When flying, try to get a nonstop flight. Avoid flying in bad weather. Think about where the exits are and what to do in case of a crash. Be prepared.
20. Maintain a "security" frame of mind—just because you're a tourist does not mean you are in a cocoon. *Just because you're a tourist means you're more at risk.*
21. Watch out for Gypsies . . . (no kidding).

20

Spousal Abuse

If he wants to kill you, he will

In violence, we forget who we are.

—Mary McCarthy

The "cycle" of abuse against women begins with a tranquil period, then tension begins to build up within the abuser and it gets to the point where there is a need to let off the pressure; an incident occurs that would ordinarily be seen as minor (the woman cooks the yolk in an egg, drops a glass, etc.); the incident triggers a violent reaction from the abuser and he strikes out, physically and mentally battering her. After the explosion the pressure is released and a period of tranquillity begins again . . .

Because the abuser feels guilty and remorseful, begging forgiveness and promising everything will be all right in the future, he may be more romantic than usual, showing his love and buying a gift. She believes him because she loves him and does not want to lose him.

Then the tension starts to build again . . .

As time goes by, the stages within the cycle get shorter until the angry abuse is followed by ever-briefer periods of calm. As the fuse gets shorter and shorter, the "honeymoon" phases, those periods in which the abuser is remorseful, began to fade and in its place is a tense silence with an undercurrent of rage on the part of the abuser. The wife and children slowly get beaten down, and the woman begins to believe that she is the one at fault—if only she had put more meat in the sauce, kept the kids quieter, paid that late bill sooner . . . a never-ending list of "should-haves," self-doubt and guilt.

Abuse really isn't about the victim—it's about the abuser and his need to rage. But why do so many women take it and stay around for more?

I'm standing in a courthouse corridor. The woman I'm talking to has a face that someone has used for a punching bag. The right side of her face is red and puffy and there are finger-sized black bruises on her neck.

"I tripped on my three-year-old's toy truck and fell down the stairs," she says.

She says it with a straight face and without sounding rehearsed.

Her husband is in the courtroom waiting to be arraigned on a spousal battering charge. It is the third time he beat the crap out of her, and she made a frantic 911 call. It was the third time she told the police, her husband's lawyer, and the prosecutor that she fell and injured herself. The woman has twice tripped up the justice system by claiming her original call for help was a mistake, and she had injured herself. When that doesn't sell, the next line of defense is that she started the fight with her husband.

This is not a rare scenario—many of the spousal-abuse

cases I've seen fit this pattern, in which the wife takes the blame for the injuries.

Fortunately, in many cities, the police and prosecutors have developed a "policy" that after one or two attempts by the wife to take the blame they go ahead and prosecute the husband. In addition, many areas now have mandatory counseling programs in lieu of jail sentences for first offenders.

We all wonder what motivates these women to protect the bastard who beats the hell out of them. Blind love? Fear of being abandoned with a houseful of kids? Such little self-esteem that they think they *deserve* it? (Don't reject the last motive as dime-store psychology—someone very close to me, who had been sexually brutalized as a child, acted as if she was dirt and deserved to be beaten and only let men into her life who kicked the hell out of her.)

There is a fallacy that abuse, and a woman's tolerance to it, is something you find only among poor people. The truth is that it happens at every level of society. A sad story that always has gotten to me was told to me by a young woman whose mother was abused by her husband during their entire several-decades-long marriage. Her father, a successful businessman, would take her mother into the bedroom and shut the door and beat her while the girl sat outside the door and cried.

Can love survive beatings? Repeated beatings? Can love really exist if it comes with violence?

Spousal abuse works in both directions, with men being victims also, but the vast majority of these cases involve men abusing women simply because a man is usually physically stronger than his wife.

I have two observations to make about spousal abuse after dealing with a number of abusers and the abused:

1. A guy who knocks around his wife is sick and should

get help (along with a little jail time, if nothing more than weekends, to get his attention).

2. A woman who sticks around for the abuse should also get help.

When you are faced with abuse from your spouse, I would advise you to call 911 and a divorce lawyer, in that order. You can get counseling after you have the law between the two of you. Anytime he gets aggressive, you give him "911 therapy" by inviting the police out. Okay, he's going to lose his job, and maybe you won't be able to pay the rent because he's in jail. But you have the rest of your life to deal with jobs and landlords. When you give in to an abuser, you are not costing yourself money but your quality of life and sometimes life itself.

Never let him get away with one punch without being punished. The first time he hits you, get the hell out and call 911. If you can work things out, fine, but don't let him have a free hit because he will have learned nothing from your passive behavior except that he can get away with hitting you.

The usual process for dealing with an abusive husband is to get a restraining order.

If he violates the order, he gets thrown in jail. That is enough for most of these jerks. But like every other situation, you get an occasional screwball who is willing to go all of the way. "All the way" means they are so nuts they are willing to kill or maim the spouse and go to jail for it. When you are dealing with someone this crazy, someone willing to go to prison for the pleasure of harming you, you may be dealing with someone whom a restraining order won't protect you from.

Don't take that statement to imply that you should not get a restraining order. *You absolutely should get one—* most police agencies will listen to your complaints and respond much more firmly and faster against the nightmare person in your life if you have a court order. But don't make the mistake of falling into a comfort zone behind a restraining order. *If he wants to kill you, a piece of paper will not stop him.*

The courts can help, the police can help, counseling, common sense, family, and friends, all can help—but do not get a false sense of security because you know you are right and have the law on your side. Spousal abusers are *criminals,* and criminals break the law. Sometimes with tragic consequences for all involved.

There is "high-tech" help for some abuse victims if you are in a jurisdiction where it is available and can bear the cost if there is a charge. Sometimes the cost of these high-tech items can be borne by the abuser under a court order, paid for by the courts if there is a program for it, or even donated by suppliers.

One piece of equipment is the "panic button" discussed as part of an installed or do-it-yourself home alarm. If he breaks in, you press the button and either send off a blast of noise you hope your neighbors hear, or, if you belong to an alarm service, the alarm company will send out the police.

Another device is a cellular phone. This can be used to call 911. There are inexpensive cellular phones on the market that only dial 911. In some communities these phones are distributed by law-enforcement agencies to abuse victims.

There is an automated system in some hundreds of communities across the country that automatically notifies women when their abuser has been released from jail. The system calls the woman and keeps calling every couple of hours until the woman responds that she got the message.

There is also a "hot-zone" bracelet similar to the house-arrest electronic devices that notify the police when someone under house arrest leaves home—only this device warns the victim if the abuser gets within a designated distance from the victim's home or work. If the abuser enters the designated zone, or cuts off the bracelet, he triggers a signal that notifies the victim and the police.

Certainly, none of these electronic miracles are going to do any good if the abuser simply wants to kill you. But with the limits our civilized society puts on doing unto others before they do unto you, they are at least something more than nothing in your arsenal.

The bottom line is not to buy into the cycle of abuse. Get out and get help at an early stage. Don't reply to violence with more violence because you will simply make yourself more of a victim. Let police officers, counselors, and courts deal with his aggressions.

21

Rape

Any female may become a victim of rape. Factors such as extreme youth, advanced age, physical homeliness and virginal life-style do not provide a foolproof deterrent or render a woman impervious to sexual assault.

—Susan Brownmiller, *Against Our Will*

When Susan Brownmiller was writing her classic thesis on rape, alcohol was the major "date-rape" intoxicant. Today we have designer drugs that have taken acquaintance rape into new dimensions. And we have an escalating violence in terms of stranger rape that has to be met with more security awareness.

Twenty years ago rape-crisis workers were cheering a substantial *rise* in reported rape cases. That sounds strange, but there was logic and humanitarian concern behind the attitude and the statistics. You see, the clinic workers did not see the statistics as indicative that there was an increase in the number of rapes, but as an increase in the number of women willing to come forward and report the crime.

Women had been intimidated by the system, a system where the law threw open their personal lives to be examined under a microscope in a courtroom; there was an attitude that if you wore a short skirt, a tight blouse, or had a couple drinks, you probably "deserved" it or at least invited it.

Attitudes and laws have changed. Today women are protected from being turned into the instigator, especially in the case of stranger rape. There has been enlightenment that rape is an act of violence committed by mentally ill criminals whose main intent is to exert power and inflict pain on a woman. Laws in many states even protect women from spousal rape. But it is still estimated that less than half of the rapes that occur are reported by the victims. Of those reported, about 20 percent, one out of five, are stranger rapes—and about *80 percent of the time the victim is "acquainted" with the rapist.*

An acquaintance can be almost anyone known to the victim—coworker, someone they dated, spouse or boyfriend, fellow student, neighbor, etc.

The two types of rape—*stranger* rape and *acquaintance* rape—involve two radically different approaches of security concern. Rape, no matter how you define it, is not an act of sex but an act of violence. Rapists are sick mentally, not oversexed. Studies of serial rapists reveal that many of these crazies were sexually molested when they were children. The major difference between stranger rape and date/acquaintance rape is that the former generally results in more physical injuries.

There is a common denominator between the two types of crime, stranger and acquaintance rape: Too many women become victims by not being security smart. When you wake up in the middle of the night with a creep with a knife by your bedside, there is little you can do. But too many intelligent, hardworking people who watch their diet, exercise regularly, and plan for the future are careless about locking the bathroom window or won't invest ninety-nine cents in a piece of window-locking hardware.

This isn't a simple world, and certainly not all stranger rape occurs because of unlocked windows or because one jogs out of sight of others. Even with the best-laid plans, bad things happen to nice people. But bad things happen *more often* to nice people who are careless about their security than people who are not careless.

Women from all walks of life are victimized by rape and the key security measure for women is not to contribute to an already-terrible situation by being careless.

Stranger rape involves the wrong place–wrong time syndrome, invasions of residences, attacks in parking lots, and the like. Security awareness is discussed throughout this book—security devices at your residence, keeping aware of your surroundings, being selective about where you park and shop, using some sense about when you park, avoiding jogging and walking at odd hours and places, having a personal security device—in essence, getting security conscious and staying security conscious.

The most important thing to keep in mind about stranger rape is that the rapist is an opportunist who is waiting for a woman to create the opportunity: a woman at night class walking alone back to her car, a woman walking from the bus or subway stop at night after work or entertainment, a window left unlocked. You cannot eliminate all possible eventualities—but you can reduce the odds greatly by giving more thought to your security. If you are going to be walking home late at night, if you can afford a taxi, take one; if someone is waiting for you at the residence, call ahead and have them watch for you or meet you partway; if you drive a car, know how to change a flat before it happens; talk to other women at school and go to and from dark areas in groups.

Having a "noisemaker" in your hand with your finger on it when you have no other backup is another security-smart attitude.

Rehearsing what you would do in an emergency—screaming and running are the first line of defense, striking at the rapist's eyes if he doesn't have a knife or gun is also in order, but don't ever get yourself into a mood of self-confidence and put yourself somewhere you shouldn't be because you took a karate class or you have a noisemaker. I frequently hear women saying that they should kick a man in the balls if they attack. That's a good theory, and I don't want to discourage any woman from trying it, but it's not as easy as it sounds or that the movies make it look. The best line of defense is *always* not giving some slimy bastard the opportunity to take advantage of you.

I believe the best protection for a home is a good alarm system. A system with a panic button by your bedside beats having a gun or mace any day. As explained in the section on home alarms, you can have one professionally installed or pick one up at an electronics store that will provide you with basic protection for most homes and apartments.

Date and Acquaintance Rape and the Drugs of Choice

Date/acquaintance rape involves the same sense of security consciousness, but the concerns take a different slant. By being aware of who the typical assailants are, who the typical victims are, and where most of these rapes take place, you will gain some understanding about how they can be avoided.

First and foremost, alcohol plays a role in most date/acquaintance rapes (although, as discussed below, a couple of designer drugs have entered the field in the past couple of years).

Men who become intoxicated are more likely to commit acquaintance rape.

Women who have become intoxicated are more likely to become a victim.

Traditionally, the hot spots of acquaintance rape are the college campuses.

About 90 percent of the date/acquaintance rapes on campus involve sports teams and fraternities.

Get together a group of young men, put them in a house or apartment where they are out of sight of the public eye, booze them up and add some women, and you have all of the chemistry for most of the rapes that occur on college campuses.

The target for the majority of these college rapes are freshmen women, many of whom have become intoxicated, some for the first time in their life. The most likely candidate to rape them are fraternity pledges who have been drinking and assault women to the cheers of their older fraternity brothers.

Keep in mind that the above are "typical" situations, and there are many exceptions to the rule. A woman can become the victim of rape on a campus from a classmate giving her a ride to school, an instructor meeting with her in his office, or in a thousand other scenarios—but the *risk* is higher and the frequency of rape is greater if the victim drinks at a party involving a sports team or fraternity.

Date/acquaintance rape involves a past history between the parties, or at the very least, involves some volitional conduct, even if it is nothing more than being alone with the man. Many of these men do not believe that they are "raping" a woman by forcing sex on her. In terms of athletes, these guys may believe that their campus "star" status entitles them to special privileges and that the woman is consenting by drinking and partying with them. (Who said these guys were supposed to have any brains?)

Personally, I do not believe that frats and jocks who gang-rape, date-rape, or party-rape, or whatever you want to call it, are just a bunch of macho young studs who got sexually aroused by booze and females and just joined in because it was the thing to do at the time. I have been in college and in the army and I know what sort of group mentality guys get into when they start drinking and talking dirty and getting aroused. But *the ones who are going to gang-bang a woman are sick people.* Just because they didn't jump out at the woman from bushes in the dark and all the "other guys" were doing it, not only doesn't make it right but proves something really is wrong with the guys who participate.

It is estimated that about 20 percent of the women who go to college become the victim of date or acquaintance rape. That's one out of five women—an incredible statistic. What is even more incredible is that only a small number of the incidents are reported. This may be changing, however, because of the awareness programs that concerned groups have formed in many colleges and universities.

However, just when society has gained awareness of the seriousness and brutality of the date/rape problem, something comes along to throw a curve in the system.

The something is really two somethings: date-rape drugs called ruffies (Rohypnol) and GHB.

The drugs affect a woman in two ways: (1) They take away the will to resist and fight back, and (2) they wash away memory of the assault.

The drugs can be used on any woman but are particularly popular on college campuses.

The best defense against a date-rape drug is to watch your drink. That is harder than it sounds because if you are in a bar and get up to go to the rest room, you are not going to carry your drink with you. And if you have gone to the man's apartment and he is fixing drinks, or even opening a beer for you, the drink will probably be out of your sight at some point.

If somebody wants to get a drug into your drink, it is going to be hard to stop the person under ordinary circumstances.

The best defense against a date rape is to try and not get yourself into a position where you have to watch your drink because you have dated someone planning a date rape. That is easier said than done, of course, because date rapists don't wear signs and women don't make men go through a battery of psychological tests to see if they are perverts before they go out on a date.

But you can have some discrimination about whom you date, how much you drink and where you go with the person. If there is anything about the person, or anything about the situation (such as going to the person's residence to drink), that disturbs you . . . don't do it. Think about what you are doing and follow your instincts. If anything turns you off, politely walk away from the potential problem.

And if you do suspect that you have been drugged and raped, report it immediately so that tests can be done and evidence preserved.

22

The Internet

A Stranger in the House

Never love a stranger.

—Stella Benson

The greatest danger of the Internet is that it can let a deadly stranger into your home under the guise of a friend. Internet crime is the fastest rising crime in America, and it is the one most of us are the least prepared to deal with because it is a strange new type of crime. Can you imagine how successful serial killers like Ted Bundy would be if they had had access to the Net? You had better start getting used to the idea of developing a security awareness because this generation of crazies do have access. . . .

There are a certain number of crazies in this world, a certain percentage of thieves, murderers, rapists, and con artists. Fortunately, most people, most of the time are nice, honest, hardworking souls. But there is a certain amount of slime anywhere—some of the people we work with, have as neighbors, buy shoes from, bump into in dark alleys.

Some of this crud has gotten onto the Internet, giving it a reputation as a wild and crazy place that it doesn't fully deserve, but there are predatory pedophiliacs lying in wait to lure young people to shabby motel rooms, rip-off artists selling phony merchandise or simply collecting credit-card numbers to exploit, porno peddlers, some doing it for the money, some doing it to get their kicks, Internet versions of the perverted phone caller who get it off 'whispering' dirty things, lonely-hearts predators who take advantage of people financially and physically—and no doubt there's a Jack the Ripper and other serial killers stalking the Internet.

When the FBI does a sting operation and an agent goes out over the Net as a fourteen-year-old girl, the chat room lights up like a Christmas tree.

People tend to be consistent—dishonest people rarely get stung by the honesty bug, gullible people tend to be suckers. The people on the Internet who rip-off others, do child porn, and stalk women, are going to be doing those things with or without the Internet, and there will be victims regardless of whether the Internet exists.

The fact that a mass-suicide cult (remember *Heaven's Gate?*) had a web site does not mean that every organization with a religious bent on the Internet is a house of crazies, but it does send a signal that not every organization on the Internet is *rational.*

There are special concerns about the Internet because the Internet creates *trust* in people. People who would be cautious of an ad in the personal column of a magazine or a telephone call from a stranger can become *disarmed* with Internet communications because a rapport between the criminal and the victim can be built up over a period of time without the victim becoming suspicious that the person they are dealing with is a con artist or worse.

It is a sense of camaraderie that Internet users are in the same "club," and the "familiarity" and friendship that builds up between Net buddies, that can make the Internet a dark and dangerous street for some people. There are "chat" rooms on the Net where almost anything goes—there are people who have "love affairs," virtual sex and all forms of stimulated fantasies, extramarital relations, and sometimes even what some segments of society would characterize as perverted. The love and perversions are all electronic, but there is a thin line between virtual reality and the real thing. The trouble begins when people cross the line after they lose sight of the difference between virtual reality and the real thing.

The Internet has thrown open the doors of our homes to *everything* and *everyone*. While that includes an incredible range of marvels and excitement, there are snakes in any Eden. And because these snakes can come into our house and tap into our minds and that of our children under the pretense of being invited guests, we have to take an extra precaution in dealing with them.

With adults, the solution is to take the same sort of caution with Internet "friends" as you would with other strangers. Parents are supposed to teach kids not to talk to strangers, not to accept gifts from strangers, not get into a stranger's car, and so on, a lot of "not to" prohibitions about dealing with strangers.

Yet interacting with strangers is exactly what kids and adults do when they sit down and start "chatting" on the Net. Conversations lead to friendships. Friendships lead to physical interaction. And that can lead to danger because no matter how much "chatting" you've done on the Internet, no matter how many secrets you've shared, how much you think you know about your Internet pal, all you know is exactly what the person wants to tell you.

Young people have to be taught that you can't trust a stranger just because you've been chatting with the person on the Net. No matter how long and how often you "chat" with someone over the Net, that person is still going to be a *stranger* to you because that type of communication brings out only the side of the person that they want to reveal.

A characteristic of many serial killers has been their ability to be charming bastards who lure their victims to them. It is all the more easy to do it electronically where the person is hidden inside a computer screen and you cannot see and hear the real person.

Another characteristic of serial killers is that they are good liars. Serial killers commonly are able to pass lie-detector tests because they have no conscience about the horrible things they have done.

Can you imagine how successful a charming, handsome law student like Ted Bundy would have been at luring women to him on the Internet?

Too many people, including teens, desperately seeking friendship or romance, can become easy victims to someone who holds out a kind hand, especially when it's being done electronically. You can't control access to the Internet—shut it down at home and your child will go to a friend or one of the coffee bars that are offering Internet access. The best approach is to try and guide your child through the problem rather than trying to make it forbidden fruit that the child may be even more tempted by.

And perhaps before we put all the blame on the Internet, we ought to look at our own lives. Happy, well-adjusted people are less likely to be lured to danger on the Internet than people desperately seeking love or approval. Children who run away to an Internet pal probably are runaway candidates even without the Internet. The Internet is likely not the root of the problem, but just a symptom. When our children suffer from the victim mentality, they become easy victims for Internet stalkers.

Many people treat the Net like the Wild West, where everything and anything goes, but the truth is that the Internet is subject not only to existing laws but to many special laws. Things that were not legal before the Net have not been made legal by it. Child pornographers may have more access to each other because of the Net, but that does not make their nasty hobby any more legal.

If you have a reasonable basis to believe that you or your child has been victimized by someone on the Internet, or threatens to be, you should report the matter to the police.

The response from the police may not be the most enthusiastic in the world if there is no dead body or missing body to go with the complaint, but if enough reports come in, the police will soon be able to compose files on Internet criminals and track them. Most federal and state police agencies have a growing awareness and concern about Internet crime.

There are some "watchdog" organizations on the Internet that try to guard against child pornographers and other crazies on the Internet. One of the organizations is called the Cyber Angels and tries to operate on the Internet much like the Guardian Angels function on the streets. Sometimes these organizations can either help with a problem on the Internet or, just as importantly, can guide you to a place where you can get help.

The FBI maintains a group that deals with child pornographers and other Internet criminals, and if you or someone you love is a victim, the local office of the FBI should be contacted. That office can refer you to the FBI task force handling the problem.

In regard to purchases, make sure you are dealing with a reputable firm before you make a purchase or give anyone your credit-card number. There are Internet services that can lead you through checking out many firms. If you have any doubt at all, make the entity provide you with information that you can check out.

Some Internet providers furnish security that prevents your on-line connection from being tapped. Don't sign up with a provider that doesn't provide security.

The Federal Trade Commission has also gotten into the act with trying to educate consumers about Internet fraud. Contacting the closest FTC office may gain you information about some scams.

If everything else fails, use some common sense: If you don't know whom you are dealing with, or can't verify that they are legit, don't deal with them. Period.

And if it sounds too good to be true—like earning thousands of dollars licking stamps at home, or buying electronics or trips to Tahiti at ridiculous prices, stop and remind yourself that there are no free lunches.

If it sounds too good to be true, it probably is. . . .

23

Protecting Valuables

For I don't care too much for money,
For money can't buy me love.

> —John Lennon, Paul McCartney
> "Can't Buy Me Love"

I have one piece of advice for people who want to protect valuables—don't do it at the expense of your life. While the advice seems like common sense, people forget it, and a great deal of the violence that bloodies our streets arises from inappropriate responses to thieves who *might* be satisfied with just taking *things*.

I have to begin this section with a confession: Protecting valuables would not be high on my list of priorities except that I might lose my life because of the way I handled protecting my valuables.

In other words, I try not to handle my valuables in a way that endangers my life.

I have had a car stolen, money stolen, car broken into,

electronics stolen at my office, my house burglarized (before I put in a home alarm system), and every loss felt like a personal invasion of my life by some slime.

But no loss injured me or my family, and that is the important part to me.

Things are often insured, are usually replaceable, or can be done without. But life is precious. You only get one chance, and it would be a sin to waste it on a wristwatch or a car.

What amazes me is the number of people who got themselves killed or someone else killed squabbling with a thief over a purse or a wallet.

Violent crimes have doubled in the past twenty years and the rate of increase of violent crimes is five times that of crimes against property. Today, Jack the Ripper would hardly make the front pages, much less history, for killing five women.

The violent crime rate is about 1 for every 150 people in this country. That means that if you live in a community of about 150,000 people, about 1000 people in town will be the victim of violent crime this year.

The rate for property crimes is about 1 out of 20. Out of that same community with 150,000 people, about 7,500 will be the victim of property crimes.

You have twice as much chance of being the victim of a violent crime than dying from heart disease, and three times the chance of being the victim of a violent crime than dying of cancer.

And almost all that crime in those shocking statistics relates to the fact *someone wants something that someone else has.*

There is a great scene in the movie *Grand Canyon* (isn't that an unusual title for a movie about Los Angeles?) in which Steve Martin, playing a big-time movie producer, is accosted in a parking lot by a guy with a gun. The robber demands Steve Martin's expensive watch and Martin, to really pacify the guy, hands him the keys to his $100,000 car. The guy shoots Steve in the leg, telling him he had asked for the watch.

I don't know what the moral to the story is. I don't know even if there is a point to the story. I guess you can say the moral is that if you meet a guy in a parking lot and the guy has a gun (and doesn't have a badge to go with it), and the guy wants your watch, don't offer him your car. Just give him the damn watch.

But it drives home a point that I have tried to make throughout the book. *The last thing we want to do is not listen carefully to a guy with a gun.* Remember the tragic story of my neighbor who turned around to go back into the house when the thief told him to hand over his wallet?

There is no question that we should protect our valuables, not only because they belong to us and any invasion of them is an invasion into our private life by trash, but because the less care you take of your valuables, the more susceptible you will be to a crime of violence. Not to mention what hell it is to deal with insurance companies after you have been ripped off.

But protecting our valuables *with our lives* is not smart.

People deal with crime against property in many ways, none of which are totally satisfactory. They insure the property and find out later that the insurance only covers a fraction of the value, not to mention a big deductible; they mark the items with their name, chain computers to a desk, hide their jewels—and find out that thieves still find them. With all we do there are still over twelve million crimes against property each year.

With the proliferation of video cameras, you should videotape your possessions. Not just your valuables, but *all of your possessions.* Not to protect them against thieves, but for dealing with an insurance company. Keep in mind that if your house or apartment burns, and you have insurance, you will have to account to an insurance company for every pair of socks, every pair of underwear, besides major items.

The one simple way to do that is to take a video of your possessions (even if you have to ask over a friend who owns a camera) and put the video in a safe place *other than your residence.* The problem with leaving the video in your residence is that it will burn up or melt down in the fire. Stick a video in most fireproof home safes and it will still melt down in a fire. Your best bet is to keep it in a safe deposit box at your bank or leave the video at work or give it to a friend or relative.

Alarm systems work miracles against crimes of property.

Dogs, especially ones with big snarling teeth or even big barks, are ounces of prevention.

The bottom line to crimes against property is that the more sloppy you are in protecting your property, the more sloppy you will be in exposing yourself to physical danger.

Take care of your property as if you are protecting your life . . . because you may be doing exactly that.

24

Reaction Time
The Quick and the Dead

Heroing is one of the shortest-lived professions there is.

—Will Rogers

That you or a loved one will be a victim of crime during your lifetime is a statistical certainty. Being street-smart and avoiding making yourself a victim includes taking fast action when crime happens. You will only be able to react quickly if you are prepared by having the right state of mind.

When I was in the army, my bayonet instructor was a short-tempered guy of Japanese descent who stood on a platform and would scream at us, "What kind of bayonet fighters are there?!"

We would shout back, "The quick and the dead!"

Then he would scream, "What kind are you?!"

"The quick, Drill Sergeant!"

Having a fear of flying, and having to fly very often, I remind myself of this phrase every time I am waiting for takeoff on an airplane. I listen to the lecture about how we are supposed to wait for instructions from flight attendants in case of an emergency (such as a *survivable* crash on takeoff and landing) and I tell myself there is no way I would hang around the plane to wait for a flight attendant to tell me when I can use the emergency exit.

It is not that I do not trust or respect flight attendants—the bottom line is that the *quick* get away from many crashes before the plane explodes.

There is obviously a difference between being *quick* and *panicking*. Panic is blind and stupid and just increases the danger to you and those around you. And there are some instances where just having quick motions can get you killed—as it did my neighbor who spun around to go back into the house when he had a shotgun trained on him by a robber.

But my theory of survival for planes, trains, and automobiles is that you react quickly to danger. I have a real bias against people who sit around with thumbs in their mouth while physical danger erupts. I have even more of a bias about people who react blindly to danger. (How many horror stories have you heard about fire breaking out in a crowded night club and everyone getting toasted because people stampeded for the exit?)

Somewhere between moving too slow and moving too fast is moving *expediently*—and that place is a matter of attitude.

People who in their own minds do not consider themselves as cattle, as part of the herd, are likely to act like cattle—blindly or slovenly—because they simply have never been trained in handling danger.

How do you develop an attitude of being expedient? By setting out some objectives and consistently following them. As you're swinging that car door shut, you lock the doors.

When you step into your hotel room, you check for emergency exits. When you make that plane reservation, you request an aisle seat near an emergency exit. (After getting seated, have you ever glanced at an emergency door to see how you open it? It might help to know something about how one of those doors are opened before a split-second hesitation can cost your life.) When you need money in the evening and the only safe ATM is inside a grocery store and it will cost you a couple bucks to use the machine, you pay the money.

What's an expedient attitude toward flying?—thinking about what airline to use (avoiding discount airplanes and charter flights using old planes), requesting seats near exit rows, avoiding stopovers, planning your vacations so you do as little flying in winter weather as possible.

If you find yourself in a crowded night club or a dark theater, take a second to help save your life by just looking to where the exits are located—before you have to stumble around in the dark, smoke, and panic, trying to remember if the exit door is to the right or left or behind you.

Have you thought out how you would react if an intruder came into your house? What are the escape routes? Would your neighbors call the police if you broke a window and screamed?

None of this should be a drag because none of it takes any serious energy or thought. All it takes is an attitude of being security conscious.

Americans are often characterized by much of the rest of the world as being soft. That accusation is not that far from the truth because it is life's experiences that make you street-wise and street-tough.

It is difficult for many Americans to conceive why they should be security conscious because they live in a country where it is reasonably safe coast to coast, border to border, but it shouldn't be difficult to conceive that *most* of the rest of the world is a dangerous place.

And it shouldn't be that difficult for the average American to realize that the secure womb they have been raised in has rapidly deteriorated. Every category of violent crime has taken an astronomical rise in the past several decades and the drug-abuse rates exactly match those skyrocketing statistics.

Like any other emergency situation, we can't wait for the sky to fall before we figure out what we are going to do. You cannot anticipate your reaction if you are sitting in a car waiting for a friend to come out of a McDonald's with a couple Big Macs and someone sticks a gun against your head. Hopefully you will have enough sense to sit quietly (although I wonder what the gunman would do if you simple *fainted?*). Just as you can't anticipate your reaction if the earth opened up and swallowed you as a result of a killer quake. But not all quakes are killers (and people in earthquake areas take preventive measures to survive quakes) and not all crime hits so suddenly as a gun to the head. And when your mind goes blank with that gun to your head, if you have conditioned yourself to stay calm in an emergency, that training will kick in.

Preventive measures are to prepare us for those situations that we have some control over. Choosing where you park at night and locking your car doors are things you have control over. It may not be enough when you are unlucky enough to run into a crazy with a gun and an uncontrollable craze for a fix . . . but it may also be just enough prevention so that the crazy goes for someone else. (That's a terrible thought—that the killer I avoid may kill someone else, but without being the least facetious, if we are going to take turns dying, you can go ahead of me.)

No one can be expected to anticipate every possible

emergency, but you should at least have thought out the common ones. Thinking your way through how you would handle one type of emergency will help you handle a hundred different ones because emergencies usually have some common denominators.

And don't forget one critical aspect to being prepared and reacting expediently to a situation: observing what everyone else is doing. If panic hits a movie theater because people suddenly start smelling smoke, don't make a mad dash for the exit until you calculate whether you are going to be trampled to death. Or end up as one of the bodies piled up in front of the door.

Give some real thought to what you should do in household emergencies because you and your family are more likely to become the victims of an accident than of crime, yet most people have very little knowledge about even the basics of dealing with accidents. Other than calling 911 or running outside, do you know what to do for electric shock? Drowning? Bleeding? Heart Attacks?

Dead Heroes Are Dead Forever

We are only given one life, and we need to conserve it and get the best use out of it. If you are going to sacrifice your life for a good cause, at least do it for someone you love and who will gain *life* themselves by it and not for a car or a wallet.

In our personal lives few of us get a chance to be a hero and even fewer can handle the opportunity when it arises. There is nothing wrong with that—it's called life.

Where I would draw the line is being "heroic" about property.

The only objection I have to heroism is that I strongly object to me or anyone else giving their life for anything but *life*. I can think of no better reason to give my life than to save someone I love. But I draw the line at giving one fingernail, one tiny scrap of skin, to save a necklace, an earring, watch, purse, a million dollars or any other damn thing that a killer wants and can be replaced.

If there is any time the *Dollars vs. Life* equation is tilted in the favor of life, it is the situation where one chooses whether or not to stop a thief from getting away with something. *Let them have it.* It may not be the most "heroic" thing to do, but it beats losing your life for $23, a hairbrush, lipstick, and three credit cards.

A sad incident occurred when a waiter, leaving work at night, walked out into the parking lot and was accosted by a man with a gun who told the waiter to give him his car keys. The waiter had worked a lifetime for the privilege of buying a relatively expensive car, and he told the man to screw off. It cost the waiter his life. It was courageous of the waiter to stand up for his rights but tragic that he did it with a crazy who had a gun.

People have lost their lives over much less than a car.

The premise I live by is that I only have one life to live, and if I have to give it up it had better be for some good reasons besides money.

Your best option (other than getting the hell away from trouble fast) in almost any situation is to call 911 for help.

That presumes that human life is not in jeopardy. What you or I should do if human life is in jeopardy is going to depend on each of us and the situation. In this gun-ridden society, life is more likely to be threatened by a gun than anything else and, lacking movie magic, the practicality is that there isn't anything anyone can do except not try to increase the number of victims.

Once upon a dark and lonely night in San Francisco (in

the days when I roamed the streets wide-eyed and innocent), I heard a woman screaming for help. I ran around the
corner to come to the rescue (I was younger at the time, and
my bones broke less easy) and saw a woman standing over
a man.

She was a very big woman and he was a very small man.
And she had a purse that would qualify as a lethal weapon.
The man was on the ground and each time he tried to get
up, she'd hit him with her purse and knock him back
down . . . and then *she* would yell for help.

From the curses she was yelling at him, I realized that he
was her boyfriend and that he had spent her booze money
before she got to it.

I left the lovers to their mating ritual . . .

Machoism Kills

Society has changed, and the aggressive people we have to
deal with are often brain-fried by drugs or stress, desensi-
tized to violence by movies, and own a gun. Machoism
("machismo") doesn't work—worse, it's dangerous and makes
victims not only of ourselves but those we love as macho reactions to crazies get out of hand and end up in violence.
Machoism is baggage from another time, and we have to rid
ourselves of it.

In the early part of the book I related a story about "Jennie and Jack" and the incident in which Jack took on a
crazy and Jennie ended up in a wheelchair. No one likes to
take abuse from a crazy, and maybe Jack had a right to fight
back. *But he did not have the right to involve another person.* Machoism doesn't just kill the person exercising the
privilege but innocent bystanders, some of whom might be
a person we love.

I am not using "machismo" in terms of its classical definition, as a strong sense of masculinity characterized by aggressiveness, domination of women, virility, and physical courage. In terms of our personal safety, I am using it in the limited sense of replying to aggressiveness with aggressiveness, whether it's telling noisy people to be quiet in a theater or flipping the bird at some jerk on the road.

Many women are guilty of this type of machismo—flipping the bird, honking their horn, or telling people off, but men are much more likely and more aggressive about acting out their rebuttal to a crazy. And much more likely to make victims of themselves and their loved ones.

We all need a realistic view of the world. Few of us can handle a serious physical confrontation. None of us can handle a confrontation when the other person, who may be six inches shorter and thirty pounds lighter, pulls out a gun—or is on a drug like PCP that gives the person the strength of several men.

The rustic state of Washington, which still has more trees and rivers than people, last year had over eleven hundred incidents of road rage, some of which were fatal. The biggest, toughest lumberjack (or computer nerd, considering that the Seattle area is now Silicon Valley North) is helpless if some crazy goes nuts and starts shooting.

Washington is just being used as an example, but the bottom line is this: The proliferation of guns and drugs has radically changed the climate for physical and verbal confrontations. My unscientific but life-experience diagnosis is that long-term drug use short-circuits the part of the brain where our inhibitions lie, making it easier for us to kill without need or regret. Throw in too much stress, so much movie and TV violence that violence is no longer "real" anymore, and you end up with a society in which one-third of the cars on the road have a gun on the front seat . . . and a stressed-out, violence-numbed and frequently drugged-out nut at the wheel (or on the street, or in movie theaters, or at school).

Most of us learn early in life that you cannot win with a "drunk." Drunks don't have control over their physical or mental actions and when we push back or fight back, they are liable to fall down and crack their head and we end up charged with manslaughter.

If you don't already know it, you not only cannot win with a crazy, but the consequences of tangling with one is much more severe than tangling with a drunk.

Take that premise—*you cannot win with a crazy*—then *don't tangle with one.*

It's that simple: Walk around a crazy, walk away from the crazy, keep your mouth shut to the crazy, don't buy into his irrationality.

I know there are people who sorely need to get the meanness and craziness kicked out of them. But everyone I have represented who set out to give some creep his just dues ended up victimizing themselves or someone they love.

25

Self-Defense

Savage is he who saves himself.

—Leonardo da Vinci

People who defend themselves with an inappropriate use of force make victims out of themselves by exposing themselves to criminal charges.

I consider myself a decent person. When I was a kid, I worried about the starving Africans and Asians despite the fact (or maybe because of the fact) my mother and us kids were sometimes homeless and hungry right here in America. I have helped many people both in my personal and professional capacities without demanding money. I am the kind of friend people call when they are in trouble or their car breaks down in hell. I am kind and generous to pets and kids (unless they bite). I capture spiders and other bugs in the house and carry them outside and release them rather than kill them. I cannot watch sad movies, and I get emotional if I am forced to watch one (I'm not joking). I would walk away from any physical confrontation that I could do

272

so without suffering great bodily harm myself. I believe in truth, justice, and the American way. (I am not being facetious.)

In regard to most of the traits above, I think I'm pretty average because most of my friends think about the same way (although they all kill spiders in the house). In other words, I am a pretty average, reasonably decent person trying to survive in a world of stress and crime.

And if someone tries to harm me or my family I will kill the bastard first if I have the chance.

Anyone who doesn't believe they are morally entitled to kill *in defense of human life* isn't taking the ultimate responsibility for their life. The whole idea is to *protect your life and that of your loved ones.* That does not mean you kill without legal cause—it means that when the chips are down and some crazy bastard is going to kill you or your family, you blow the bastard away (or stab, bludgeon, or do whatever else it takes).

Anyone who would rather give their life or a member of their family's life rather than see some street trash bite it should go into a holy retreat and be spoon-fed.

By killing in self-defense, I am referring to defense of *life,* not property. If you are a macho dude and see nothing wrong with stepping out of your house to blow away with your deer rifle the punk kid who is driving off with your favorite pickup, you have wasted your money on this book because you either are, or will be, part of the problem with crazies in this country.

The reference to killing in self-defense is being made specifically to defense against criminals who are out to kill you or your loved ones. That doesn't include mama-papa fights, leaving someone's teeth marks on your car bumper if he flips you the bird, or shooting the occasional teenager who runs out of a liquor store with a six-pack of beer. And, as a notorious New York City case illustrates, it doesn't include pulling out an illegal weapon and blowing away youths who are giving you a bad time on the subway no matter how much you may feel they deserve it.

What it means is exactly what it implies—that you take a violent criminal's life to save an honest life. Frankly, we have an excess of violent criminals in this country, and having another rot in hell won't cause me to lose any sleep.

The Laws of Self-Defense

The laws of self-defense vary from state to state—but there is a *common thread* to most laws: An innocent person can in self-defense counter deadly force with deadly force.

That does not mean you can get in a pissing match with your neighbor and blow him or her away when the neighbor starts shouting threats and insults or even waving a garden spade at you. It means exactly what it should imply to you: If some dirty bastard intends to use deadly force, you can use deadly force in self-defense if you have no other choice.

In that regard, make sure *you* are not the dirty bastard who started the problem and brought it to the point of the use of deadly force.

And if you can retreat, do so. Most state laws require you to retreat if you can.

Almost all states take a dim view of shooting people while they are running away (assuming they are not covering their retreat with gunfire), shooting people you know (it's a lot harder to explain why you killed your spouse or a neighbor than a guy wearing a ski mask), and killing someone who couldn't have carried out the threat (make sure the gun the kid is carrying fires real bullets and not water).

A general theme in the law of self-defense is that the actions are judged by what a "reasonable person" would have done under the same circumstances. However, while the courts provide some guidelines, "reasonableness" commonly ends up as a question for a jury to decide. (Remember, you don't get to a jury until you've been arrested and charged and lost several inches of your intestine.)

Use of Force to Defend Your Castle

Resisting an intruder in your home is obviously high on the "reasonableness" meter of judges, juries, and police officers.

Within limits.

Shooting someone you've had a history of problems with, gunning down your ex-spouse or your drunken brother-in-law, even when they are banging at your door, isn't going to generate much sympathy unless you can show a clear danger of the risk of death or great bodily injury.

This doesn't mean you have to let someone kick in your door and come inside your home and kill you. But your chances of being arrested and charged with murder go up astronomically if you kill someone you know.

Again, the standard you will be judged by is what a reasonable person would do under the same or similar circumstances.

The Bottom Line on Self-Defense

The best defense in most cases is getting the hell away from trouble as quick as possible. *Physical self-defense is for a last-ditch, cornered-rat effort that should be applied only after running, screaming, or calling 911 has failed.* But when your back is to the wall and you have to defend yourself against an unprovoked attack that could cause you great bodily harm, strike back as quickly as possible, as hard as possible, and get away as fast as possible.

The real bottom line on self-defense is to make all of the noise you can, run if you can, fight with everything you have if you can't run. Never give up. Never stop fighting. Never stop trying to escape. You only have one life. Don't waste it by being a lamb led to slaughter.

But don't overact to a situation and end up making yourself a "victim" because you have killed someone, or end up in jail for punching someone in the nose who sorely needed to be punched. You don't win with a crazy, and with today's negative attitudes about self-defense, the police usually arrest both parties to a mutual-combatant situation and let them pay through the nose for lawyers.

Guns: Ignoring Them Kills You

You do not have to love guns or own guns, but we live in a nation in which there are more home guns than home computers, *more guns than people,* so you better be ready to deal with them.

Even if you hate guns, fear guns, or have no use for guns or for the people who have guns, you cannot afford to stick your head in the sand and pretend that guns do not exist.

Guns do exist. They are unsafe. We would have a better world without them. Owning a gun places you in jeopardy. It increases your chances of being involved in a suicide, homicide, burglary, or accidental shooting. *But guns are out there by the tens of millions, hundreds of millions, and we have to deal with them.*

276

Even if they are not in your house, they are almost certainly in one—or both—of the houses next door.

You may not have a gun in your car, but a car next to you may.

You may not have had a gun in your hand, but it is inevitable that sometime or other you will be in the company of someone with a gun (hopefully not a cop cuffing you or a crook holding you up).

I have represented dangerous people who have used guns violently on others and who have used them in self-defense. I have had a gun in my hand. I have had a gun pointed at me. I was threatened by a crazy who claimed he was going to kill me and then killed himself instead. Most of my relatives own guns.

Guns are dangerous. Thousands of people are accidentally shot each year. Many thousands more are *deliberately* shot. Kids find them in closets, under the mattress, on an impossible-to-reach top shelf. They find them and kill themselves and others with them.

In terms of personal safety, guns are generally useless because either the gun is not handy or the bad guy already has you in the line of fire. The third scenario is that he got to your gun before you did.

In terms of home security, guns are highly overrated. You're liable to come home and find the thief with your gun in their hand. Or come awake with a gun or knife at your throat before you have a chance to reach for your gun. A gun in the house creates an unjustified sense of confidence. If I had to make a choice between a gun or an alarm system, I would choose the alarm system.

Types of Guns

Regardless of whether you own a gun or never plan to own a gun, you should be familiar with guns. The following information will give you a very general idea of what guns are about in case you or your child encounters one.

There are several broad categories that most (but not all) household guns fall into.

First, there are *rifles* and *shotguns*. The laws for buying, possessing, transporting, and owning a rifle or shotgun are generally less strict than for handguns. It is not that rifles and shotguns are less dangerous than handguns—to the contrary, rifles and shotguns have much more fire power. (Do you recall that during the infamous North Hollywood bank robbery shoot-out, cops ran to a gun store to borrow rifles because their 9mm pistol bullets were bouncing off the robbers' body armor?)

The reason handguns are much more controlled than rifles is simple: Handguns are concealable.

Handguns come in two general categories: *semiautomatics* and *revolvers*.

Revolvers are the guns you've seen in Western movies: those pistols that the cowboys and gunslingers wear holstered low on their hip and refer to as "six-guns." (A revolver gets its name from the fact that the chamber holding the bullets, usually six bullets, revolves as you pull the trigger.)

Just because you have seen them in movies about the Old West, do not make the mistake of categorizing revolvers as old-fashioned or out-of-date. To the contrary, revolvers have been the most popular gun among police officers in the country until the last several years when fears of being outgunned by criminals have driven many cities to give officers the option to carry a semiautomatic. Many officers still carry a revolver as a backup to their semiautomatic.

The reason for the popularity of revolvers is the simplicity and reliability of their operation. You simply pull the trigger and they fire. On the other hand, semiautomatics take more action to get them to fire. "Cocking" is the process of getting the weapon into a mode where it will fire. A revolver does not have to be cocked before you pull the trigger because it cocks itself with the pull. A semiautomatic has to be specifically cocked before pulling the trigger the first time it is fired, unless the semiautomatic is the type called a double-action semiautomatic—that weapon cocks like a revolver as you pull the trigger.

Once cocked, the semiautomatic is capable of being fired faster than a revolver. Viewing the two guns in a very simplistic way, the trigger to the semiautomatic (once cocked) is more of a "hair-trigger" than that of a revolver and thus can be fired faster.

So why has the revolver been the traditional choice of police officers and many gun owners? Because there are two problems with the semiautomatics: They occasionally jam and are more likely to go off accidentally because the trigger is easier to pull.

I want to emphasize again that if the purpose of owning a gun is home protection, for the same money you can buy an alarm system that is much more effective and much less dangerous.

26

Dealing with the Police
Surviving the "attitude" test

The terrorist and the policeman both came from the same basket.

—Joseph Conrad

Knowing when to keep your mouth shut is the most important thing you need to know about dealing with police. With the rise of drugs and gangs, police work, especially in metropolitan areas, has become similar to combat. Like other combat personnel, police officers get hardened and shell-shocked. If you want to get the police on your side, you need to understand police officers and keep some basic rules in mind in dealing with them.

I have dealt with many police officers: as a victim of crime, as a suspect in a crime, as an attorney defending people accused of crime. I have even represented police officers accused of crime. I have seen police officers lie on the witness stand (so often that criminal defense lawyers refer to officers' testimony as "testi-*lies*") and I have watched officers risk their life to save mine.

Overall, I believe police officers deserve more credit than they get. I know they can be hard to deal with. Almost every interaction I have had with police officers, other than the one in which officers risked their life for me, has been unpleasant. But I believe I understand police officers, and I certainly have great respect for them. The fact that so many of them have kept their sanity and their spirit of duty and commitment to service is incredible considering what today's police officer has to put up with.

In big cities, many police officers remind me of battle-fatigued soldiers. Street cops often spend their duty hours rushing from one crisis to another. There has been a proliferation of violent crime—that means police officers have to tackle more dangerous criminals, more police officers are killed and wounded. In the inner city, gangs outnumber and outgun officers whose handguns and shotguns don't stand up well against gangbangers with assault rifles. Anyone who hasn't had to get down and dirty with street trash has no idea of what a tough and dirty job a cop has.

No matter what you think of police officers, whether you support them (as I do despite some negatives) or hate them (which is pretty stupid), you have to deal with them, so you had better understand a couple of critical factors about dealing with them.

First, these men and women are under terrific pressure. Some are a bundle of stress and raw nerves. And they take crap all of the time, mostly from the street trash they have to deal with. So when they deal with Joe and Jane Citizen, if you get in their face you are liable to get slapped.

Because officers have to deal with so much physical and verbal aggression from criminals, many of whom are irrational, the worst thing you can do with a cop is be aggressive.

That does not mean you have to take crap yourself—it means you remain calm and try to express yourself in a reasonable manner rather than screaming at the cops who are investigating you or the incident you have reported.

There is no question that the squeaky wheel gets the grease, even with the police. But it is definitely a time to squeak rather than screech. I have handled many cases in which my client, the innocent party, ended up being the one getting arrested because he or she could not keep his or her mouth shut when the cops arrived.

Even when you know you are in the right, try to remain calm and get your point across so that the cops don't come to the conclusion that you are the problem.

And don't try to rub it in when you are right. Remember, these guys have badges and guns and take crap all day.

A few years ago I represented a successful businessman who had been busted for drunk driving in the past and hated the cops for it. Late one night he got stopped by the cops, only this time he was sure he had them—he had not had a drop to drink. He jumped out of his car and confronted one police officer on the driver's side while the other officer approached on the passenger side.

He proceeded to tell off the police officer on his side of the car, letting him know exactly how he felt about the police.

My client was rather small in size, and the police officer was rather large.

The officer picked the guy up and threw him over the car to the other officer, who promptly cuffed him and dragged him back to the patrol car.

He was charged with interfering with an officer in the line of duty. That's a very vague charge that usually means the cops don't like your attitude. It is a serious charge, and it means you have to hire a lawyer and defend yourself. The charge almost always arises when the only witnesses to the offense are the officers who charge you, so it is hell to prove your innocence. What happened to my client was very unfair, but he stepped into it by opening his mouth at the wrong time. He turned himself into being a victim in a situation that he could have kept his mouth shut and walked away from.

Too many people get excited and make fast movements when dealing with police officers. The ordinary citizen isn't usually in danger of getting shot just because he is agitated when the cops arrive, but it does nothing for the person's credibility—or that all-important attitude.

Keep in mind that your average police officer is a very idealistic person. Police work is hard, demanding, dangerous, and stressful. The pay is not terrific. While some officers may go into law enforcement because they like guns and uniforms, most police officers are dedicated to fighting crime. But they also know that the public often has a negative attitude toward them. (It amazes me that lawyers, who *everyone* hates, and cops, who many people hate, are most often the heroes and heroines in movies.)

Police officers, especially in big-city battle zones, develop an "us-against-them" attitude in which anyone offending another officer is a bad guy. That's not uncommon in any work or sports situation, only in this case when the officer happens to be the bad guy, he or she carries a gun, a club, mace, and the authority to arrest you.

The bottom line is to deal with police officers in a reasonable and courteous manner.

Don't be afraid of calling the police. Call first, and if you are wrong, apologize to the officers.

Because of the proliferation of 911 calls, most of which

are false alarms, you may have to do some real demanding to get an officer out if the 911 operator thinks you are merely scared and not in danger. If you think you are in danger, don't take no for an answer—get it across to the 911 operator that you need help, *now*.

27

A Plague of Crime

*For my own part I would as soon be descend-
ed from the heroic little monkey, who braved
his dreaded enemy in order to save the life
of his keeper; or from that old baboon, who
descending from the mountains, carried away
in triumph his young comrade from a crowd
of astonished dogs—as from a savage who de-
lights to torture his enemies, offers up bloody
sacrifices, practices infanticide without remorse,
treats his wives like slaves, knows no decency,
and is haunted by the grossest superstitions.*

—Charles Darwin, *On the Origin of Species*

Only about one *out of every* five *crimes result
in the arrest and prosecution of the criminal.*

—FBI Statistics

Understanding who the enemy is and what makes them tick
will help you in dealing with the people who can take your
life and your property (besides the IRS).

It has been pointed out that there are nearly two million people in jail in this country. That figure bears repeating over and over because the enormity of it comes home when you consider it doesn't include the ones who didn't get caught and the ones out on bail or their own recognizance, and the ones who are in between committing crimes.

The bottom line is that there are a lot of mean-spirited people out there, many of whom have drug-fried brains.

I have dealt with every type of criminal I can think of, from murderers to weenie wavers, and criminals in general fall into a few categories with some common traits: They all have antisocial behavior, are losers, and either do not believe, or do not care, that their actions hurt others. Some of them are violent, some of them can be violent under the right circumstances, and some of them are nonviolent.

There are three generalities about "criminals" that you should be aware of because it affects them and affects you:

1. Most criminals remain consistent throughout life. That means they don't change. If a person commits a violent robbery at nineteen, there is little chance he will not be inclined to commit a violent robbery at twenty-nine and thirty-nine. It's true that some criminals are rehabilitated and become wonderful citizens. But they are the exception, not the rule.

2. Most criminals are not afraid of going to jail. Because so many of them are unable to cope with ordinary demands of everyday life, (like paying rent and holding down a job), they unconsciously welcome jail. That means that the punishment they face for a crime often will not deter them from committing the crime.

3. Drugs pay a significant role in street crime and burglaries. Long-term drug use alters reality and judgment. The brain of the criminal pointing a gun at you may be so drug-fried that he has little or no control over his actions. One of the more shocking stories I've heard is the death of a twenty-five-year-old pregnant woman who was shot by a druggie at a busy ATM machine in a nice neighborhood in broad daylight. She didn't resist—he simply shot her and took her money in front of witnesses. There was no reason to shoot the woman—but there is no *reason* in a burned-out brain.

If there is any question in your mind whether we have an epidemic of crime in this country, you must be visiting from another planet.

To survive an epidemic of crime, you have to get yourself into the survivor's state of mind we talk about throughout this book, and you are not going to do that unless you have some notion as to how widespread the disease has spread.

There are about 1,800,000 violent crimes committed in this country every year (that includes nearly 25,000 killings, 100,000 forcible rapes, 600,000 robberies, and over 1,000,000 aggravated assaults). Robbery is theft through the use of force or violence and aggravated assault is an intent to inflict severe bodily harm.

There were over 12,000,000 property crimes (such as burglary and larceny).

There are about 1,700,000 men and women in jail or prison at the present time. Think about that figure—*one million, seven hundred thousand people.* That is more people than the combined populations of the states of Vermont, Delaware, and Wyoming.

Two-thirds of that 1.7 million are doing *hard time in prison.*

The prison population *more than doubled* from 1985 to 1995.

Prison sentences in the 1950s were about twice what they average today.

Today, the average time served for *violent crimes* in general is about three and a half years (violent crimes include murder, kidnapping, rape, robbery, assault, etc.). That is three and a half years—not decades, not eons, but a measly three and a half years. That means a criminal going to jail at the age of twenty (and the majority are under the age of twenty-five) would be twenty-three years old after serving the average time for a *violent* crime.

That's about the same amount of time it takes to get a college degree—a *Bachelor of Violent Crime* degree.

The average time served for *homicide* is five years, eleven months. That includes murder and less severe intentional killings (such as voluntary manslaughter).

The same person who went in at the age of twenty would be twenty-six years old when he or she got out. About the same amount of time it takes to get a graduate degree—a *Master of Violent Crime* degree.

Think I'm being facetious? I've been in a lot of state and federal prisons (fortunately only as a lawyer). I've even attended the prison wedding of a man convicted of two killings. I've represented hundreds of men and a much smaller number of women who have done, are doing, or probably will do hard time. Full-time public defenders after a few years can number their clients in the thousands. And few would disagree with me that in prison mean people learn to be meaner.

Let's take a look at some more statistics:

- Men account for over 90 percent of those incarcerated. That means you have more to fear from men than women. But women are getting more and more involved in violent crime as they follow the path of men in drugs and gangs.
- Over 90 percent of the White victims were killed by . . . White offenders.
- About the same percent of Blacks are killed by . . . Black offenders.
- While it is true that traditionally people are generally killed by persons of the same race, with interracial marriages becoming more and more common, and spousal violence still so prevalent, this statistic is being eroded.
- On the average, about three-quarters of the offenders are men. (Are women more honest, less violent—or are they just smarter and get away with it more?)
- And about three-quarters of the murder victims are men.
- Historically, the majority of murder victims knew their killer. In other words, the killings usually involved family, friends, or neighbors. But that statistic has changed for the 1990s. Now the majority of victims are strangers (or there is no information about a previous relationship or other connection).
- The biggest murder rate is for males in the 20 to 24 age group. About 75 percent of all killings are of people 17 to 44 years old.
- Over half of all criminal offenses are committed by persons under 25 years old.

- About 75 percent of all murders are done by firearms, with the vast majority of those committed by handguns.
- If you are going to be killed by someone in the process of committing a felony (rape, robbery, burglary, etc.), it will most likely be during a robbery—about half of the murders committed during the commission of a felony arise out of robbery.
- There are nearly 3,000,000 burglaries a year. About two-thirds of all burglaries were residential in nature. About two-thirds of all burglaries involved forcible entry. About 60 percent of residential burglaries occur during the daytime. The burglary rate is slightly higher in the summer than winter. Some burglaries end up as robberies when the resident arrives home to stumble into the burglary—or is simply home when the burglar breaks in. Some burglaries also end up as murder and rape.
- The most frightening statistic of all is that violent crime has nearly *doubled* during the last two decades. Do not let that statistic fly by without thinking about it: That means that twice as many criminals are resorting to violence than in the recent past.
- In that same time period, property crime has only gone up about 20 percent—in other words, violent crime has increased *five times faster* than nonviolent crimes.

Criminals are simply more and more casual about killing their victims. Why? The reasons that jump out are drugs (criminals are much more whacked-out than they used to be), the widespread possession of handguns, and the desensitization about violence that movies and TV have spawned.

If those statistics do not frighten you, think about how many people are in the process of being recycled back to prison after being released and committing more crimes.

Prison is a revolving door.

Criminals are a recycled commodity in our society.

These are not just figures and statistics. There are real people, real pain, death, and losses behind the statistics. There are millions of victims behind the statistics.

And there is something you personally can do about the crime statistics in America: Don't add to them!

PART IV

Protecting Children

We watch them, these children of light, going forth into the world every day and trusting so simply that they will not be harmed. They are the blessings we count on, even as they count on us. By protecting them—and by training them to protect themselves—we are assuring our own psyche survival.

—Roderick Townley, *Safe and Sound*

28

**Abuse, Molestation,
Self-Protection**

ABUSE: The same cycle of abuse described in the chapter on spousal abuse applies to children, but the situation is much more serious because a child is more fragile and helpless and often gets the abuse from both parents.

MOLESTATION: Children are the sexual toys for older children and grown-ups—not just pedophiles who are strangers but from family, friends, and neighbors. The child has to be taught to understand molestation and report it.

SELF-PROTECTION: Perverts and killers prey on children, and our children must be taught how to handle themselves and *protect* themselves because children are grabbed off the street or from the front yard, not out of your arms.

Abuse

Anyone who has spent any time in a child-dependency courtroom has had their faith in mankind—and womankind—rattled. I have never heard of nor have I seen in print or on TV horror stories to match what I have seen in this type of case. What parents, stepparents, grandparents, siblings, and the people next door can do to small children, often their *own* children, isn't fit to print or show publicly. These courtrooms are not open to the public to protect the privacy of the child. Perhaps they should be thrown open to the public because they are America's dirtiest secret.

Child-dependency courts deal with the protection of children who have been abused, molested, or abandoned. During the proceedings, prosecutors and attorneys represent the child and parents. Personally, I cannot handle these cases anymore. I have close friends who consider it their professional duty to handle these cases, but I can't stand dealing with a man or woman who has abused a child. I can look a guy in the eye who has backed out of a liquor store shooting it out with the owner, but the parents who abuse their children are not just criminals, they are sick and repulsive (not all of the cases are this bad—I represented one set of parents who had been arrested for having a dirty house!). There are enough seriously repugnant cases to turn your stomach.

Many of the children in the dependency courts got their injuries as a result of the same type of "cycle of abuse" set forth in the section on spousal abuse. But there are major differences. A battered spouse is able to seek help. A battered child is a prisoner—to both parents because *both* are guilty—a mother or a father who stands by and lets a child get abused is as responsible as the abuser. The child is trapped, not just financially and emotionally, but is physically unable to escape the abuser because it's someone in the household—someone they love and are afraid to hurt or "tell on."

And often worst of all, a child will be emotionally scarred by abuse and carry the trauma through life and to his or her grave. Another tragic consequence of child abuse is that abused children sometimes grow up to be abusers themselves. Eighty percent of abusers claim they were abused themselves as children. Abuse can make a child have terrible feelings that may become the road to raging violence against others. (The "generational cycle of abuse" is well known to police and counselors. It can be the most powerful and terrible inheritance that a child gets from a parent.)

The cycle of abuse begins with the parent calm. Over a period of time, for some people it may be almost daily, for others months go by, stress builds up in the person. It may be stress from work, family life, or the person may just be the type who can't handle life. The stress becomes more and more intense and the abuser needs to release it. The child provides the trigger by doing something—wetting his or her pants, breaking a toy, making noise. The stimulus can be almost anything because the child's actions are not the cause of the stress. The abuser explodes and strikes out at the child.

After the explosion, the abuser is calmer. And quite often, even remorseful, showing their love for the child by buying a toy, hugging the child, and telling the child that mommy and daddy love him or her. Everything is fine because children are very forgiving and the abuser has released the tension.

Then the stress starts to build again . . .

Children who are the targets of abuse often cannot be "taught" to report the abuse because the person "teaching" the child is the abuser or is permitting it. Occasionally a social worker or teacher discovers it, or a neighbor calls the authorities, but the vast majority of these situations are something the child has to live—and die—with.

Family members and friends are often aware of these situations and remain silent because they are not completely sure or are afraid to get involved. If you are reasonably certain that a child is being abused, a call to your local child-protective agency, even done anonymously, may save a child irreparable harm. With one phone call, the process of stopping abuse can be started because the abuser will know "someone" is watching.

If you are aiding and abetting abuse because of your own fears and weaknesses, get help from professionals. There are organizations who counsel parents about abuse. Get to one and bare your heart because you may be the only hope a child has.

Abuse is a crime—but it is also a sickness. The abuser needs counseling. So does the victim. It won't go away by ignoring it.

I have to leave this with another story about my mother. Some of these stories may seem bizarre, but you have to remember that in my mother's day, things like women's shelters and family counseling either didn't exist at all or certainly didn't exist in the small towns we lived in. We were poor and uneducated, but my mother was not an ignorant woman, and, much more than book learning, she had good instincts about how to handle situations. My father, who wasn't around much, was a hard-rock miner, a harsh trade in which the men burrowed in the ground all week and raised hell on the weekends before black lung and alcoholism took them to an early grave.

My father had a violent temper, and when he drank, rather than calming it, the liquor loosened his inhibitions and he became a bastard to deal with. However, my mother protected her children from his rages. When they happened, she got us out of the house and called the police. (I can remember one time when the local marshal had to use tear gas to get him out of the house.)

One night when I was ten years old he came home drunk

and I did something to trigger him. I don't remember what it was, just something kids do, but he went into a rage and came at me. My mother heard the commotion from the kitchen and came running—grabbing a pan of water she'd been boiling eggs in. She came at him and threw the boiling water on him. It stuck in his clothes and he ran screaming out of the house. When he came back from emergency, he found his clothes on the ground outside.

Please note—I do not recommend that you meet violence with violence, let alone scalding people. It was a different world, and there was neither the recognition that child and spousal abuse existed, nor were there private and governmental agencies to help. Today the type of action my mother took might get someone killed, including the mother and child, not to mention the woman would be arrested.

The only "moral" to the story is that we have to take care of children. We have to stand up for them and fight for them because they can't do it themselves. Today you don't have to battle physically—you can dial a phone and alert a nationwide system of child-protective agencies that come to the home and deal with the problem. If someone in the household is abusing a child, don't put up with it. Get the child out and get help. And if you're part of the problem, you need to seek counseling yourself.

It is not the responsibility of the child to protect the parent. It is always the responsibility of a parent to protect and care for the child. Children are not to be sacrificed for the sake of keeping peace in the household or keeping a marriage together. We don't sacrifice our children for anything.

Molestation

About one out of four girls and one out of seven boys are molested by the age of eighteen. Like child abuse, this creates emotional scars and we know that many molesters were once the victims of molestation.

Although it is common to think of girls as the subject of molestation, boys are also targets. A little boy's body is not that much different from a little girl's body to a pedophile.

This is a subject sometimes badly handled by parents. Parents don't have any problem teaching their children not to take candy from strangers and not to get into a stranger's car, but molestation is something that can go on right under a parent's nose and they fail to see the symptoms—and have failed to train the child to report the problem.

Children have to be nurtured to deal with molestation from the time they are able to respond to it by letting a parent know it has happened. In dealing with children, the parent has to be aware of and use appropriate methods of instruction gauged to the child's level of sophistication. A parent starts the process by teaching the child about the child's body and letting the child know that only the parents have the right to touch it—and that there are limits to what even a parent can do. "No one touches the parts your swimming suit covers" except doctors and parents (and then with limits).

The child has to be taught how to deal with other people who touch them and to understand the limits on the touching. Children are often used to being passed from hand to hand and fondled by a wide range of people—even complete strangers to the child will pick up the child at a social gathering and give it a hug or a pat on the fanny. Parents commonly make a mistake by training their child to be friendly with someone who the parent may love and trust but is a "stranger" to the child. Old friends, aunts and uncles and grandparents, who live a distance away and with whom the child has had little contact, may be a "stranger" to the child. While these people may be absolutely trustworthy, we make a mistake of pushing the child into their arms at first meeting because it gets the child used to being handled by someone unfamiliar to them.

When the child is meeting new people, don't push him or her at the person by immediately letting the child be hugged and kissed. Let the child warm up slowly to the person at the child's own pace. Let the child know that they have rights, that they are not a "toy" for bigger people to play with or fondle at will.

By giving the child "rights" in regard to good people, they will be better prepared to deal with bad people.

Teach the child acceptable sexual behavior—that they don't talk about, touch, or grab private body parts. A child needs to learn to respect their body and defend it, but not be ashamed of it.

People who molest children control the child in a number of ways. They do so by instilling a sense of love or trust in the child . . . or fear. It is not uncommon for a molester to tell a child that its parents or siblings (or even a pet) will be killed, or that the child will be blamed, if the secret is revealed.

Often children carry the shame and guilt of what has happened to them as if it were their fault. Children are overwhelmed by the molestation. It is not uncommon for the child actually to have a traumatic memory loss from the situation. A parent has to lay a foundation to support the child emotionally so that the child will come forward with the problem and be able to deal with it. Again, depending on age and sophistication level, a child has to be told that any act of molestation has to be reported to them, regardless of the source, and even if there has been a threat that the parents will be killed or other harm will happen to the parents or the child if it is reported.

There are some "clues" that may alert you to the fact that there has been a molestation. Children, especially after the age of eleven or so, have a certain amount of sexual curiosity and exhibit forms of sexual interest and behavior. Behavior that is too sophisticated for a younger child may be an indication that the child has "learned" this behavior as a result of molestation. The education could have even come from an older child. Sometimes children who have been molested will act out the molestation with other children.

Abrupt changes in behavior or symptoms—excessive or unusual masturbation, redness in private areas, discharge from a girl, yeast infections in a young girl, bed-wetting, high degrees of anxiety, fear or avoidance of another person such as a neighbor or family member, abrupt shyness or anger, are sometimes indications of molestation (and, of course, any one of them could be innocent).

If you suspect molestation, don't "spoil" the evidence. Ask just enough "open-ended" questions to ensure that your suspicions are reasonable, then seek professional advice. An "open-ended" question is one that solicits a response from the child rather than feeding the child the answer: "Can you tell me what has upset you?" "Why is there a mark here?"

The problem with you dealing with the problem yourself is that the police and courts know that a child can often be easily persuaded and influenced. *Children have a tendency to give you what you want*—if you ask them if Daddy molested them, and you are going through a divorce with Daddy and have been bitter toward him, the child might say what you want to hear. Say it enough, and it becomes real to the child.

There is one last piece of advice, and you will not find it in a textbook. It was given to me by a woman who raised four children and as a professional counselor, has dealt with hundreds of molestation incidents: Be careful selecting a baby-sitter and avoid using teenage boys as sitters. She is not slamming teenage boys—the world is full of wonderful teenage boys. She is merely cognizant of the fact that boys and girls have different sex drives and that there is a greater incidence of teenage boys molesting a child (boy or girl) than a teenage girl. In other words, she is playing the odds because a baby-sitter has "open season" on younger children. Even the nicest of young boys have very strong sex drives and are curious about those strange new feelings.

Self-Protection for Children

Teach a child to protect its life. It's the only life the child will ever get.

These are the best of times and the worst of times for young people.

They are on the edge of a future of what may be unlimited breakthroughs in science, medicine, entertainment, and employment—but it is a scary world in which there are threats that have not existed since barbaric bands roamed the countryside to rob and kill; a world in which a single terrorist with a nuclear weapon could not only destroy a great city but set off a chain reaction that could launch a nuclear holocaust that could destroy life as we know it; a world in which relationships between people are fluid, with many people taking a lease on love rather than buying marriage and family, in which sex is readily available and potentially lethal.

It wasn't very long ago that people worried about whether

too many sweets would rot their children's teeth. Now there is more concern about the child sticking drugs in their mouth that can fry their brains.

As I mentioned earlier, I have had the unfortunate duty as an attorney to represent parents who abused children and at other times representing children who were abused by their parents (or others). The difference in the type of abuse that was occurring when I first became a lawyer and that which is routinely before the courts today is nightmarish. Crack, crank, movie violence, stress, alcohol, whatever the causes, the effects are devastating. Parents (along with girlfriends, boy-friends, relatives, and neighbors) do things to children that are sickening and repulsive. Some of those abused children grow up to be abusers themselves. Some even go on to major-league stuff, serial killings and the like.

The world has changed for all of us but it changes most rapidly for the very young because they don't have the reference of years to compare the changes with. If they are going to survive the future, they need as many tools as we can give them.

Many parents and all grandparents were raised in a much simpler world . . . the threat of nuclear destruction was there, but it was in the hands of a few governments; gangs were in our cities, but drugs had not made gangbanging into a megabusiness; they carried switchblades instead of assault rifles (and Hollywood did musicals about them, showing them dancing and singing in the street with switch blades—have you ever heard of someone doing a drive-by shooting with a switchblade?).

If you are not security conscious, for whatever reason, you are not going to raise children who are security con-scious—that means that the first step is to get the right atti-tude within you to pass it on.

There are two aspects to security and children:

1. *Protecting the children*
2. *Children protecting themselves*

Most parents are reasonably well equipped to protect a child when the child is with them. There are horror stories of parents letting a small child wander away to be molested or worse, even in fast-food restaurants and crowded gambling casinos, but children are generally safe with their parents—*as long as the parents themselves are safe*. When you go to that ATM at night or fail to lock the bathroom window before going to bed, you put yourself and your children in danger.

Problems that arise can vary so much you cannot cover all of them. As mentioned earlier, being security conscious is not creating a laundry list of every conceivable situation that could arise because you cannot cover every possible situation and will most likely be in shock when the situation does arise. Rather, *it is a state of mind that you take with you throughout life*. You pass those traits on to your child by way of example.

A rule of thumb for parenthood is that security-ignorant people raise security-ignorant kids. Your kids are not going to learn how to lock car doors, the bathroom window, request a second-floor motel room, and check the motel windows unless they see you do it. *By way of example and redundancy, you become security conscious and pass on the trait to your children.*

One major attribute every young person should learn is when to say "no."

Kids are encouraged to say no to drugs, and they should be encouraged to say no to security threats. There was a horror story a few years ago about two young people, a young man and a young woman, both college students, visiting the Mardi Gras in New Orleans. They stopped their car to ask directions of two men on the street, and the men offered to get in and show them the way. Instead of showing them the way to the celebration, the young people were forced to a remote area where the girl was raped and both were murdered.

One reason why this tragedy occurred is because these young people were unlucky enough to ask directions of the wrong people—killers are not lurking on every street corner waiting for someone to stop and ask directions to the Mardi Gras, but with that tragic one chance in a million, they were waiting this time. But if those young people had been security conscious, if one of them had the sense to say "no, thank you," at the critical moment when the two men volunteered to get in their car, they might be alive today. Perhaps they were too embarrassed or too inhibited to say "no." You don't have to be *too* nice to strangers. Saying "thanks" is enough. You don't have to open your doors to them.

You cannot train children specifically to react to every friendly gesture by a stranger that could endanger them, but if they are generally security conscious, when the situation arises they will instinctively say, "no."

Saying "no" at the right time is one of the most important traits a child can learn.

A recent horror story in Southern California concerned a young boy who was enticed to get close to a man who had stepped out of a van and offered money for some information. There was a group of young boys and girls, and most of them ran from the man. One boy stepped forward. His body was found later. The boy was no doubt a trusting and sweet youth.

If you can't say no, don't expect your child to be able to say it.

When you teach a child how to swim, how to cross a

street, not to play with guns, you are teaching security measures to protect the child's life. But don't stop with the obvious: People who teach their children not to swallow pills from the medicine cabinet often do not train the child to lock their doors if they have to go to a pharmacy late at night; people who read the labels on everything that goes into their mouth, shop for fresh fruits and vegetables, get the right balance of fats, join a health club to live longer and better—will drive to the health club without locking their doors, park in a dark lot and walk to the club without carrying a security device in their hand, and then go home and go to bed with the bathroom window unlocked, or fail to get a ninety-nine-cent locking device to secure a sliding window.

The fortunate thing is that most children most of the time will avoid tragic harm.

The sad thing is that so many get harmed when it could have been avoided.

More than instilling a sense of caution toward strangers, a parent has to train the child how to react in different situations. Pedophiles and serial killers are much more clever than a child—to arm the child, the parent has to "rehearse" with the child different situations and have the child act out its response. It would be very foolish to "tell" a child that they have to dial 911 in an emergency and not "act out" various emergencies and give the child practice at dialing the telephone and telling the operator the problem and address (many 911 systems have access to the address where the call originates from).

Parents and children should act our various kidnapping and molestation attempts, and other threats, and let the child get hands-on experience how they should react to the situation.

Children have to be taught to react *quickly and run* in the face of *any* threatened danger. Unlike an adult who may have some chance along the line to escape, they are less likely to get away once a predator has their hands on them. A child can often outrun a slower adult—especially if the child is able to maintain a safety zone and is taught to be alerted when strangers abruptly approach.

The child also has to be taught what to do if he or she is grabbed by a stranger. *Noise* is the best defense, but the attacker may put their hand over the child's mouth. The critical thing for the child who wasn't able to run is to physically resist by biting, clawing, running and especially screaming—making as much noise as possible. Have the child act out holding on to their bike and screaming as if someone has grabbed them and is trying to drag them into a car—act out biting and kicking.

Because we are used to seeing and hearing screaming, crying kids, the child needs to be taught to scream that the person they are struggling with *is not their parent*.

Would such conduct make a kidnapper even more violent toward the child? The sick animal who grabs a child intending to do harm to the child is going to do the harm whether the child resists or not. It's more likely resistance would give the child a fighting chance to get away or alert others rather than simply being a lamb led to slaughter.

It is difficult to train people not to freeze up in a moment of danger. But if anyone can be taught, it's kids. They have to be taught to fight back and do everything they can if they are seized. I'm not talking about fighting back against the school bully or a gang of kids who may just want to push the child around a bit. And I'm not talking about the karate classes that build confidence and little else.

I'm talking about instilling into the child the will to live, to survive, and to take responsibility for his or her own life. One frightening but necessary trait is a never-say-die mentality if the child is grabbed by a stranger—the child should resist and keep on resisting.

Susan Jones, a counselor who works with children and raised a household of wonderful kids, passed this advice on: "Amidst all these concerns as parents we still need to raise healthy children who have trust in themselves and their world. Role models create trust in others as well as precautions. Because children learn their relationship skills from parents, there is a duty upon parents that goes beyond our own narrow prejudices and passions. Set limits on your relationships, don't go popping in and out of partner's lives, but learn to wait, develop a relationship, and sustain it. Know when to stay and when to run. If there is a problem, seek help early to avoid permanent damage. Get marital therapy to learn positive skills and parenting classes to learn how to nurture a child along healthy lines. Forgive quickly but be assertive. Anger management classes can help with temper and behavior problems. Avoid drug and alcohol abuse and seek help if you have a problem. And most of all, learn to pay attention to your feelings, to that well of human instincts we call 'our gut.' Trust yourself, your instincts, and it will lead you to a safer place."

Index